JANE LONG'S BRAZORIA INN

An Early Texas Cookbook

Written and compiled by

Neila S. Petrick and Lorraine Savarese Dittmer

Illustrated by Mary Evelyn Jones

Published by Coldwater Press

9806 Coldwater Cr.

Dallas, Texas 75228

Third Printing 1999

ISBN 1-880384-0207

c COPYRIGHT 1992. All rights reserved.

ABOUT THE COVER:

The cover is a house like many built during the time of Anglo immigration to Texas. The real Brazoria Inn burned during the Texas War for Independence and no one knows exactly what it looked like. That it was plain is no doubt true. The guests slept in upstairs rooms that were long and had beds for five or six people. The Old Stone Fort now on the campus of Stephen F. Austin University in Nacogdoches is being renovated and might give an idea of what accommodations were like in the days of early Texas.

ABOUT THE 'RECEIPTS':

We could find little actually written or collected by Jane Long. Her personal belongings were lost in the fire that destroyed Brazoria during the infamous ''Runaway Scrape'' when the Texans fled east in fear of Santa Anna and his army before the Battle of San Jacinto. However, we have diligently researched the era and believe that the recipes which were in fact called ''receipts''were authentic to this period.

ABOUT THE WRITERS:

Neila S. Petrick is the author of Jane Long of Texas, a biographical novel soon to be published in paperback by Pelican Publishing. She also wrote "Woman of Texas," a one-woman drama about the life of Jane Wilkinson Long which has been seen by more than 22,000 people.

Lorraine Savarese Dittmer is a New Yorker who is an expert and inventive cook and has adopted the Southwest as her home. She makes regular pilgrimages to Santa Fe where she enjoys the marvelous restaurants.

ABOUT THE ILLUSTRATOR:

Mary Evelyn Jones is a teacher and artist who lives in Andrews, Texas. She grew up in Falfurrias and shares a love of Texas and the Southwest with the writers. All are fascinated by the women of early Texas and how they survived and flourished in a harsh land.

TABLE OF CONTENTS

SPECIAL HISTORICAL MENUS

CONTENTS (CONTINUED):

RATE OF CHARGES

Lodging and board per Week $6.00

Lodging and board per Night $1.50

Breakfast.................................. 50¢

Dinner..................................... 50¢

Supper .... 25¢

Lodging .... 75¢

Breakfast served to boarders 6:30 a.m. - 8 a.m.

Breakfast serv. to gen'l public 7:30 a.m. - 8:30 a.m.

Dinner 12 o'clock to 1:30 p.m.

Supper 5 to 7 o'clock

Sunday breakfast 7:30 a.m. o'clock

Sunday dinner one o'clock

There is no Sunday supper.

Laundry service is available Mondays. Inquire as to charges.

THE STORY OF JANE WILKINSON LONG AND THE BRAZORIA INN

From the Writings of Henry Stuart Foote in "Texas and The Texans or Advance of the Anglo-Americans to the Southwest including a history of leading events in Mexico from the conquest by Fernando Cortes to the Termination of the Texan Revolution." Vol. I. Philadelphia: Thomas, Cowperthwait & Co., 1841.

> "In the spring of eighteen hundred and fifteen, there dwelt near the City of Natchez, a juvenile belle of great vivacity and loveliness, whose wit and beauty were heightened by the refinement of her manners and the purity of her sentiments. Though young in years, she was not a minor in mental accomplishments; and attracting the admiration of all, she was wooed unwon by suitors of the highest renown. She was now arrived at that age when the laws of Mississippi require a parentless child to choose a guardian. Accident led to the choice which she made; and whether it was a prudent and judicious one, the reader must determine when he hears the sequel."
> -- Henry Stuart Foote

The history books mention her rarely. A few elementary and junior high schools bear her name. She is Jane Herbert Wilkinson Long, called by some the "Mother of Texas." She was born in Maryland, near Baltimore, moved to Mississippi when she was orphaned and lived most of her days in the territory, the independent nation and finally the state of Texas.

Anglo-American and European men came by the thousands to make new lives, some by conquest, others as legitimate immigrants in the vast land called Texas. Few women came in the early years when there were no hotels or inns. One who did was Jane Herbert Wilkinson Long, young, fearless, spiritual and devoted to an adventurer husband who ursued a doomed cause. Some say he was murdered.

Dr. James Long married the young lady, Jane, although her family did not approve. A daughter was born to them, but Dr. Long was not one for putting down roots, and soon was appointed by the citizens of Natchez to head an expedition into Texas.

Now called General Long, he arrived at Nacogdoches and took possession of the Old Stone Fort, which is there today on the campus of Stephen F. Austin University. He attempted to establish a civil government and declared the country an Independent Republic. At that time there were fewer than eight thousand settlers in the entire territory. However there were many Indian tribes that were nomadic. Some were friendly to the settlers and others simply used their hard work by taking crops and stock. Long offered headrights and bounty lands. He had with him a small military force. His wife joined him, but he immediately departed for Galveston Island where he hoped that the famous pirate Jean Lafitte would help him pay for his expedition. The minute he left Nacogdoches, the army of Mexico advanced on the town scattering the invading army from the east.

Everyone fled and eventually gathered on Point Bolivar, called Las Casas. A brief journey to New Orleans turned up more funds for Long's expedition and he lead his soldiers and his wife back to Point Bolivar. Soon, Long left Jane alone on the island and travelled to La Bahia, later called Goliad. There he was captured, taken to San Antonio and eventually Mexico City where he died mysteriously.

Still in her early twenties, Jane survived Indian attack, near fatal illness, the loss of two children, hunger, abandonment, betrayal and widowhood.

One of Stephen Fuller Austin's Old Three Hundred, Jane first farmed, and later opened the Brazoria Inn which she rented from John Austin, a cousin of Stephen's, in the new town of Brazoria.

The smart young businesswoman was driven to become a rebel in the fight for liberty against a mercurial Mexican government, itself struggling under a new flag. Above all, Jane was a powerful civilizing force in the early days of Texas, helping establish churches, health care, schools and housing.

As proprietor of the Brazoria Inn, she crossed paths with the dominant historical figures of her day: Her uncle, General James Wilkinson, Andrew Jackson, Sam Houston, William Barret Travis and Stephen Fuller Austin. She was a cousin to the wife of Ulysses S. Grant and related to other nationally prominent Americans.

To satisfy our curiosity about what foods they had, how they gathered and prepared them, and how a woman made an honorable living in a rough territory peopled predominantly with men, we travelled the roads Jane journeyed, through the deep green Natchez Trace, to Alexandria and Nachitoches, Louisiana, to Goliad and Nacogdoches, Texas, back to New Orleans, then on to San Antonio, Fort Bend, St. Augustine, Brazoria, San Felipe de Austin, Washington-on-the-Brazos, Houston and Richmond.

We found old "receipts" originating in Scotland, Mexico, France, Spain, the Netherlands and among the Indians.

We discovered worn kettles and skillets and pots, weathered bread bowls carved of wood, iron spiders that fit into fireplaces, and best of all, recollections written down more than one hundred years ago that explained to us how Jane "managed" her Inn.

She was known to have fed as many as 500 in one evening. There is a marvelous story about the night Stephen Austin made his famous "war" speech. Jane oversaw the dinner, and then collected all the guns before she would seat anyone. All of that we've attempted to pull together into a book that unifies the complicated elements of a woman's life in early Texas. That the life is Jane Wilkinson Long's, called The Mother of Texas, makes this effort all the more interesting.

A KITCHEN OF 1830

POTS AND PANS AND SPIDERS AND BRANDIRONS

While we don't know exactly how Jane Long's Brazoria Inn kitchen looked because it was burned during the infamous "Runaway Scrape," let's imagine how it might've appeared. Your eyes are drawn first to the massive fireplace in the kitchen, this one larger than most. It's where Jane and Ki cooked meals for guests and lodgers.

In England, they called this "downhearth" cooking. It meant you cooked in and around a huge fireplace. There was no freestanding stove. In Texas, the fireplaces were often huge, filling the side of a room, high enough for a small person to stand upright and perhaps three and a half feet deep. If they were well designed they had all sorts of shelves and niches and hangers which made the chore of cooking a bit easier. Since Jane had a knack for planning and organizing, we believe that she helped design her own fireplace at the Inn.

At each side of her fireplace, there might have been two ledges which sometimes cold travellers sat upon to warm themselves and at other times Ki and Jane placed pies and cakes to cook or biscuits and corn bread to keep warm.

Just above these ledges was a small bread oven close enough to the coals for bread to cook. The entire back of the fireplace is a "fireback," in some places made of cast iron, but here in Texas, heavy slate. Its purpose was to prevent the back wall of the fireplace from getting too hot and crumbling.

In front are a pair of brandirons, "firedogs" they're called abroad. They keep the big logs from rolling out onto the puncheon floor. Over these is a handy fixture with an arm to hang kettles and pots over the fire called a chimney crane or a "sway." A good one can be adjusted both horizontally and vertically.

There is also an andiron or "spit dog" for spit roasting. It has a sharp end to pierce the meat and a handle to turn the meat. When Jane wanted to catch the meat drippings, she put an iron tray underneath. To one side is a baking iron, a three-legged iron piece that looks like a trivet, but is tougher because it is often set into the fire to hold flat-bottomed pots and pans.

Brazoria Inn cooking pots likely were heavy cast iron with welded sides. The local blacksmith was a handy man, doing more than making horseshoes. The average pot size was about twelve inches in diameter and ten inches in height. A sturdy long handled frying pan was used to protect the cook as were hearth tongs for retrieving hot things from the fireplace. Vegetables and dumplings could be wrapped in muslin or net and hung inside a pot of cooking meat. Suet puddings and dumplings could be cooked the same way which made it possible to do all the meal preparation in one spot.

Other useful kitchen items included bread bowls carved from wood, copper pans, plain iron frying pans, a Dutch oven, a sugar loaf clipper used to clip off the hard sugar that came in a cone-shaped blue paper wrapper, mortar and pestle to reduce pieces of sugar, spices and medicinal ingredients, earthenware mugs and jars, a whetstone, good knives and flat griddles for cooking hoe cakes, biscuits and various candies.

While the women had some conveniences, work began long before sunrise and continued far past sunset. Indeed woman's work was never done.

BUILDING THE PERFECT COOKING FIRE

Jane Long's fireplace in the kitchen of the Brazoria Inn was by far the largest one in the town. In it, she could prepare meals for dozens of people, and if she had the time, she could manage several hundred which she did on several historical occasions. The key to a successful cooking fireplace was that the fire was never allowed to go out. Further, it was tended day and night. At times it was stoked hot, when certain kinds of cooking were being done or when water was being heated to wash dishes. At other times, the fire burned low when foods required slow cooking. Jane and Ki, along with Mrs. Ramos, Ann Wilkinson and others, learned the fine art of tending a fire. Their lives depended upon it.

They would begin with two or three thick heavy logs that required two men to put in place. Next three or four smaller logs were added and then kindling or small dried branches collected just for the purpose of building the kitchen fire.

THE FIRE NEVER GOES OUT, BUT IF IT DOES!

The fire was never allowed to go out, but if it did, every pioneer worth his salt had a tinder box, and inside it a piece of charred linen or other linen. She would strike the steel and flint causing the tinder to smolder from the spark. Next she would light a "spunk," a thin piece of wood dipped in a sulphur compound and when it flared up, she would light a candle and then the fire.

Crude as Jane's facilities were, they were modern compared to the tools of some Indian women who made good food with a wooden bowl, an iron pot if they were fortunate, water jugs and a horn spoon. It seemed to be enough. Since Eve, women have managed. It is fascinating to see just how they did.

Old San Antonio

THE SEGUINS OF OLD SAN ANTONIO

An early Texas family that made a large contribution to the development of Texas culture was that of Erasmo Seguin (Juan Jose Maria Erasmo de Jesus Seguin). He was born in 1782 in what was then called San Fernando de Bexar, later to become San Antonio. Don Seguin always found a place for travellers either at his ranch or in his home in the small city of about 3,000 people. Among his guests were Jane Long, her two daughters and her slave Kiamatia, when the group came to San Fernando to discover what had really happened to Dr. Long, Jane's husband.

Don Seguin was the first "alcalde" or mayor of Bexar. In 1812, he organized the first public school in the city. He was assigned to assist Moses Austin in his Texas colony, but when the senior Austin died, Don Seguin became good friends with Stephen F. Austin and helped him establish the first Anglo colony in the Texas territory. Later he represented the young Texas state in Mexico City after Mexico won independence from Spain. Later when war seemed inevitable, Don Seguin backed the Texas cause totally. Once the war was won, Seguin helped reestablish a stable government in San Antonio. The Texas city of Seguin is named in honor of Juan N. Seguin, son of Erasmo. Juan Seguin's story deserves an entire book in its telling.

Dona Seguin, his wife, was known for her charitable work. She was a devout Christian who spent her life serving others. It was her counsel that helped Jane Long get through the terrible cholera epidemic that took so many Mexican and Texas lives in the mid-1830s.

The Alamo
1828

DON SEGUIN'S NEW YEAR'S DAY BUFFET

Cabrito Tamales

Cured Virginia Ham

Candied Sweet Potatoes

Posole Frijoles

Flan

Fresh Oranges

Sugared Almonds

Royal Cake With Fruit Filling

Coffee

Texas Mustang Grape Wine

CABRITO

To cook a small cabrito(goat or lamb), cut off the fat and wash the meat well. Melt lard in the biggest pot you have and brown the meat. Add several quarts of water, onions, chili pods if you want it hot, and salt. Black pepper can be added. Cook for about 2 hours.

TAMALES

Ingredients:

4 lbs. pork
Chili pods
Water
1 cup lard
Dried corn husks
2 cloves garlic
Flour to thicken
6 cups masa harina
Salt to taste

Cook chili pods in water until tender. Remove seeds and stems and outer skins. Cook pork and garlic cloves in water until the pork is tender. Remove it from the liquid and retain the liquid. When the pork is cool, cut it into chunks. To the meat stock add chopped chili pods. Add about a tablespoonful of flour and stir. Put in the meat. Bring to a boil and simmer until the mixture thickens. Let this cool while you beat the lard and the masa harina together. To this you add meat stock to make the mixture soft for working. You soak the corn husks in hot water during this time. Drain them and spread a thin layer of the masa harina mixture. On top of this, you put a tablespoonful of the pork mixture. Roll the corn husk and masa mixture around the meat mixture. This is hard to do because you do not want to ruin the shape of the tamales. You can tie the ends with string, or lay them in a neat stack. You then cook them in a steamer for about an hour. Pour off any liquid and they are hot and ready to serve. Remove the husk.

CURED HAM

Soak a medium sized ham all night. The next morning cut away the rusty part from underneath and wipe it dry. Make a paste of flour and water and cover the ham with this. Put it into heavy earthen dish if you have it and cook it over a slow fire for four to five hours. Once it is done, break off the crust and peel off the skin. Dress up your ham if you are having company. Vegetables cut up and placed on it are nice. Now you can boil a ham, but slow cooking it adds to the flavor.

CURING PORK

For each hundred pounds of hams, make a pickle of ten pounds of salt, two pounds of brown sugar, two ounces of saltpetre, and one ounce of red pepper. Pack in a water-tight vessel and add four to four and a half gallons of water, or just enough to cover the hams. First rub the hams with common salt, and lay them into a tub. Take the above ingredients, put them into a vessel over the fire, and heat it hot, stirring frequently; remove all the scum, allow it to boil ten minutes, let it cool and pour over the meat. After laying in this brine five or six weeks, take out, drain and wipe, and smoke from two to three weeks.

HOW TO SMOKE A HAM

Take an old hogshead, stop up all the crevices, and fix a place to put a cross-stick near the bottom, to hang the articles to be smoked on. Next, in the side, cut a hole near the top, to introduce an iron pan filled with hickory wood sawdust and small pieces of green wood. Having turned the hogshead upside down, hang the articles upon the cross-stick, introduce the iron pan in the opening, and place a piece of red-hot iron in the pan. Cover it with sawdust and all will be complete. Let a large ham remain ten days, and keep up a good smoke. The best way for keeping hams is to sew them in coarse cloths, whitewashed on the outside.

CANDIED SWEET POTATOES

Ingredients:

10 medium-size sweet potatoes
1 and1/2cupsbrown sugar
1 cup well water
4 tablespoons fresh cream butter

Boil the potatoes in their skins and then cool. Peel off the skin and cut in halves lengthwise. Set aside. Make a syrup of the sugar, water and butter. Put the potatoes into the syrup and cook slowly over a low fire until the syrup becomes thick. Pour out into a heavy dish and pour the rest of the syrup over the potatoes. Add more butter. Serve hot.

POSOLE (HOMINY)

Wash hominy several times in cold water and then put it into a washpot out of doors over a well-tended fire that has burned down and is burning steadily. What you want is a low simmer which will make your posole nice and tender. Once the hominy is soft but not separating, you can add four or five pounds of tender cooked pork and vegetables if you like. Carrots work well. Put in garlic and two or three onions for more flavor. You'll need quite a bit of salt, but add it a little at a time and taste as you go.

HOW TO MAKE HOMINY

Hominy is a preparation of Indian corn, broken or ground, either large or small, and is an excellent breakfast dish in winter or summer. Wash the hominy thoroughly in one or two waters, then cover it with twice its depth of cold water, and let it come to a boil slowly. If it be the large hominy, simmer six hours. If the small hominy, simmer two hours. When the water evaporates, add hot water; when done, it may be eaten with cream, or allowed to become cold and warmed up in the frying pan, using a little butter to prevent burning.

FRIJOLES

This seems like a waste of time because everybody knows how to cook beans, but here it is anyway. You wash the beans in several waters and then you soak them all night in about three quarts of clean water. The next morning, pour off this water, add more water and put in one or two cloves of garlic and some salt pork, maybe two or three thick slices of it. First, bring this to a boil, but then let it simmer for nearly 2 hours until the beans are tender. Watch to add water during the cooking as you may well use up what you first put in. You can tell when the beans are tender by taking some out and mashing them with a fork. You don't want them mushy. Here is when you put in the salt, but not too much.

FLAN

Ingredients:

9 fresh hen eggs
2/3 cup sugar
3 cups fresh milk
Pinch of salt

Mix together 6 eggs yolks and 3 whole eggs, reserving the egg whites. Add 2\3 cup of sugar, a pinch of salt and 3 cups of milk. Set this mixture aside while you carmelize 1 cup of sugar in a heavy skillet and pour into individual custard cups. Pour in the custard mixture, and then set cups into a pan of water. Cook in a moderate oven for about an hour or until the knife comes out clean. This is a popular dish from Mexico that is very much at home in San Antonio.

ROYAL CAKE WITH FRUIT FILLING

Ingredients:

9 egg whites 1 teacup butter
2 teacups sugar sifted 'til fine
3 1/2 teacups flour
Teaspoon baking powder or small yeast cake
Teacup of sweet milk
Tablespoon of liquor, possibly whiskey.

Separate eggs. Whip egg whites with a clean fork. Set aside. Cream together butter and sugar. Cut in flour and baking powder or yeast cake with a knife. Add sweet milk and stir into a smooth batter. Add a tablespoon of whiskey if that is to your taste. Blend into egg whites. Turn immediately into three cake pans. Bake until lightly browned on top and a broomstraw comes out clean. The oven should be of an even heat, which might come later in the day after the heavy cooking is completed. While the cake is baking, prepare fruit for between the layers and on top. Mix 1 lb. of chopped blanched almonds, 1 lb. chopped raisins, 1 lb. cut up figs and 1 small jigger of whiskey or rum if you like it. Mix with a white icing you make from 3 eggs and 1/2 lb. sugar. When cake is cooked, spread with the icing. This makes a beautiful cake.

SUGARED ALMONDS

Ingredients:

2 cups whole almonds, blanched
1 cup loaf sugar
4 tablespoons fresh butter
1 teaspoonful essence of vanilla

Heat almonds in heavy iron skillet with sugar and fresh butter. Stir the ingredients constantly until almonds are toasted and the sugar turns a golden color. Depending on the heat of the fire, this requires from twelve to seventeen minutes. Then you add your flavoring, essence of vanilla or maybe some other if you have it. Spread the concoction out on a clean board to cool. You might sprinkle on a little salt to bring out the flavor. This'll make nearly a pound.

MUSTANG GRAPE WINE

Mustang grapes grow freely from the Texas soil, we hear all the way up into the northern part of the territory. Wait til this bounty is real ripe before you gather the grapes which will be in the middle to late summertime. Wear gloves and long sleeves when you gather the grapes because the skin of the grapes can irritate the skin and the eyes. I need barrels of wine for the guests at the Inn, so I make this wine in a whiskey barrel that I saved from a shipment. We gather bushel baskets of grapes and pour them into the barrel. It helps if a hole has been drilled in the barrel and sealed with a cork earlier. We then mash the grapes with a paddle and let them stand for a week. Set the barrel over a wooden tub and uncork the hole already drilled about six inches above the bottom. Allow the grape juice to strain into the tub through thick cloth.

Add plenty of sugar 'til the juice is almost syrupy. Pour the juice into crocks and tie muslin over the top. The storm cellar is a good place for the crocks to be out of the way while the grapejuice ferments. Once the fermentation ceases, then seal up the container. Several months is not too long for this process if you want strong sweet wine. When you put the wine into bottles or jugs, some people add a raisin to each bottle. It is best not to shake the new wine.

NEW YEAR'S EVE CUSTOM OF SPAIN

It was an old custom in Spain to eat grapes on New Year's Eve, one for each stroke of midnight that a person would have great good luck in the new year. In Old San Antone in 1824, grapes were rare, especially in January and thus the celebrants would eat dried raisins instead.

WOMEN'S ROLE IN THE TEXAS WAR FOR INDEPENDENCE

When the settlers first joined the empresarios in Texas in the 1820s, the women could use a rifle as well as the men. When war came in 1836 and 1837, the women were left alone to kill game for the family, defend against bandits and some Indians, and to run bullets for the soldiers. One way the women learned to handle rifles better was to get together for "target shooting." Such events were not uncommon, and some women simply made it more fun by providing refreshments.

As the cry for war against the tyranny of an unresponsive Mexican government grew, the women of Texas were asked to "run bullets," which meant make bullets, cut patches or wadding for the bullets and generally support the volunteer army's preparations for meeting a much stronger and better trained military force. Most of the officers of the Mexican army were trained in Europe, some under Napoleon, others under Spanish royalty. Jane Long helped in the effort by holding a combination tea and target shooting party behind the Brazoria Inn. She also hid cannon and rifles in an outbuilding behind the Inn, at the risk of her life.

Target Practice Tea

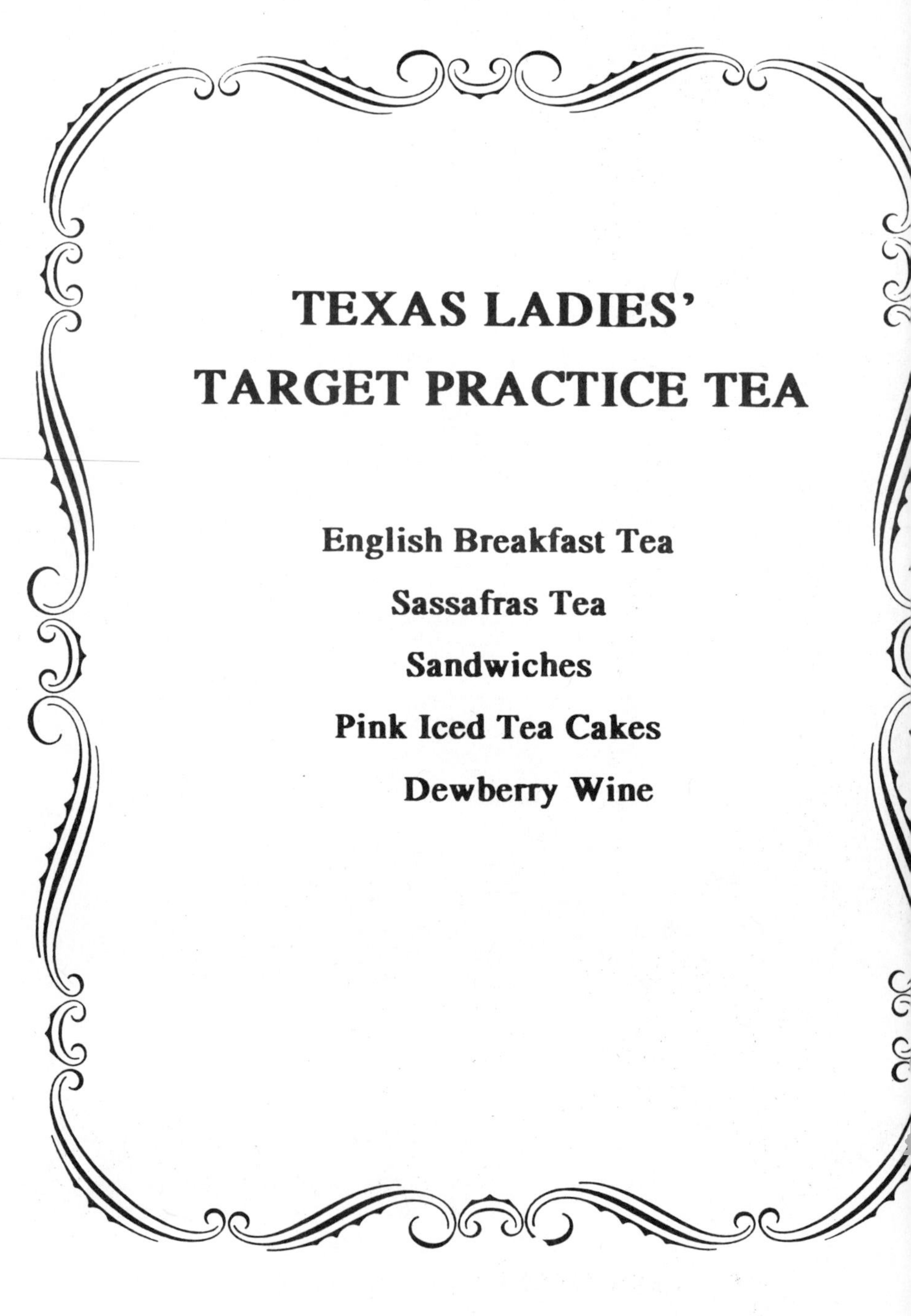

TEXAS LADIES' TARGET PRACTICE TEA

English Breakfast Tea

Sassafras Tea

Sandwiches

Pink Iced Tea Cakes

Dewberry Wine

TEA CAKES

Ingredients:

4 eggs
2 teacups sugar
1 cup buttermilk
1 cup fresh churned butter
1 teaspoon cream of tartar
Flour

The flour is to give body, but roll tea cake very thin before cooking.

Icing:

3 egg whites whipped frothy; 2 tablespoons sugar; 2 squares chocolate. Mix well and spread over tea cakes.

HOW TO MAKE COLORED FROSTINGS FOR CAKES

Pink Coloring: Strawberry or cranberry juice makes a fine coloring for frosting, sweet puddings and cakes.

Yellow Coloring: To color icing, put the grated peel of a lemon or orange in a thin muslin bag, squeezing a little juice through it, then mixing with the sugar.

Green Coloring: Take fresh spinach or beet leaves, and pound them in a marble mortar. If you want it for immediate use, take off the green froth as it rises and mix it with the article you wish to color. If you mean to keep it for a while, make the juice very strong and add to it a quart of alcohol. Seal it in an air-tight crock.

DEWBERRY WINE

Gather dewberries in the early morning. Wash them thoroughly outside and when you're done, measure out the berries thusly. Six cups of berries needs one quart of water, twelve cups needs two quarts and so on, depending on how much wine you want and what other ways you wish to use the berries. The men usually say they want to use all the berries for the wine and don't care much for the pies. Cover over your container and allow it to stand overnight. Strain the contents through cheese cloth twice. For every gallon of juice, add three pounds of sugar. Let the wine set up in a stone crock where it will ferment. This requires from two and a half to three weeks. Seal it up tight and set it aside for at least four months. Then pour it into smaller bottles and seal these shut. This is a wine that does taste better after it has set up for as much as a year or longer.

THE BEST WAY TO BREW A POT OF TEA

In early Texas, there was little to comfort a woman save a hot cup of tea shared with another woman journeying through the territory with her husband going to their new farm or ranch. Sassafras tea also was a standard for treating most any ailment. You would take a handful of sassafras roots about three inches long and scrub them clean, seeing that no bark remained. Put them into a gallon of water and bring it to a boil. Then slow the heat and let the roots simmer until tender. Let this cool, and then strain the liquid through cheesecloth. Serve hot or tepid. Another fine tea was fresh mint. Wash it several times and boil it in several quarts of water. Strain it just like the sassafras tea and serve it hot or cold.

TEXANS DECLARE THEMSELVES FREE

The place was humble, a log cabin in none too fine repair. The participants were a diverse lot, farmers and ranchers, bankers and speculators, soldiers and cotton brokers, an inventor, a poet, even a politician or two. Most had come to Texas for a new beginning, some for a new start. All had dreams of independence, the right to live and let live, the hope that they could support their families. But trouble had come to them in the form of repression. A fledgling government in Mexico City, itself uncertain in its own newfound freedom from Spain, handed down edicts, taxed, repressed the new citizens and did not allow proper representation. What was missing was a "government of the people, by the people and for the people." Rebellion was inevitable as the tide, given the nature and backgrounds of the Anglo and European settlers who joined with resident Hispanics tired of being ruled from afar.

Thus, on March the 2nd, 1836, at a tiny hamlet called "Washington-on-the-Brazos," representatives of the people but not of the government of Mexico, framed and issued the Texas Declaration of Independence. They defined the nature of government, listed their grievances and sent it to the authorities in Mexico City. War would follow soon after.

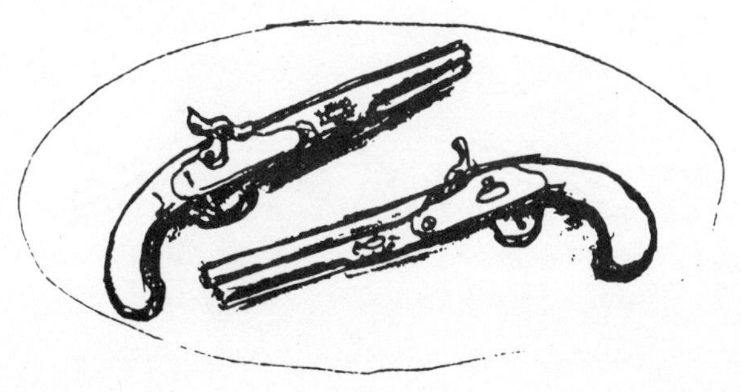

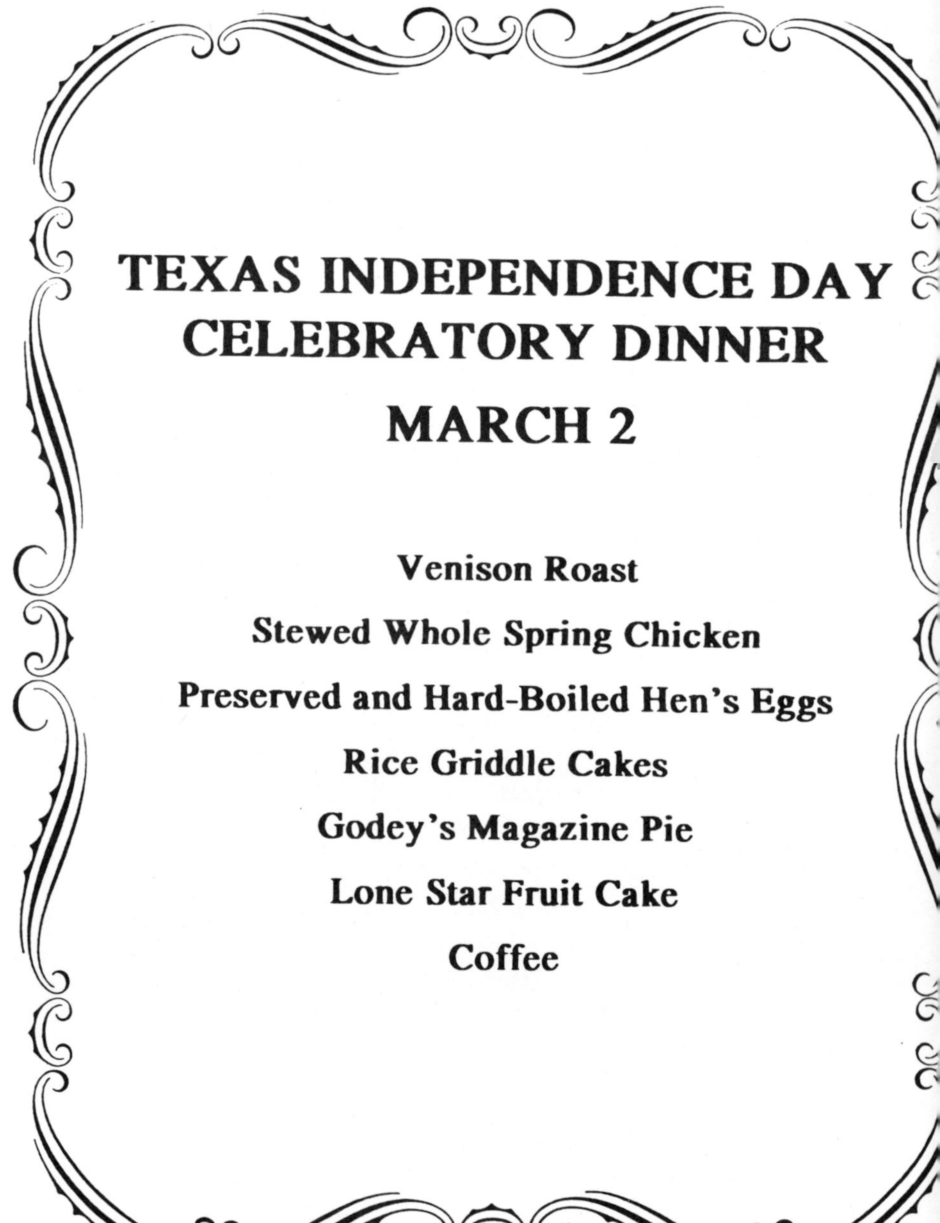

TEXAS INDEPENDENCE DAY CELEBRATORY DINNER

MARCH 2

Venison Roast

Stewed Whole Spring Chicken

Preserved and Hard-Boiled Hen's Eggs

Rice Griddle Cakes

Godey's Magazine Pie

Lone Star Fruit Cake

Coffee

VENISON ROAST

Wash the roast well. Cut a clove of garlic in half and rub it all over the venison. Flour, salt and pepper the meat. Melt lard in a Dutch oven and then brown the venison all over. Remember that venison is often dry and you must add fat when you cook it. Remove the venison roast and there will be brown liquid in the pan. Mix that with about a half cup of flour. Add more salt and pepper to taste. Stir this constantly until it is a dark brown. You begin to add water until your roaster is nearly half full of the brown liquid. Two chopped onions and comino add to the flavor. Once the onions are tender, you put the venison roast back into the Dutch oven and spoon lots of gravy over it. Then you cook the venison real slow for about four hours, pouring more gravy over it on the half hour. Add more water if you need it.

STEWED WHOLE SPRING CHICKEN

Wring the neck of a full grown spring chicken about the same size as for roasting. Pluck the feathers and singe them, and then wash the bird. Season simply with salt and pepper inside and out. Then you fill the body cavity with fresh shucked oysters. Place the chicken in a deep pot with a close-fitting cover. Set the pot into a large pot full of boiling water and cook until the chicken is tender. The meat will about fall off the bone when it's done. Warm a large platter and put the chicken on that. Then pour your gravy into a pan, add a teaspoon of fresh butter and half a tea cup full of cream. Chop up three hard-boiled eggs, various herbs if you like and a tablespoonful of flour. Let this mixture boil up and pour it over the chicken. Serve hot.

HARD BOILED EGGS

Eggs for boiling cannot be too fresh, or boiled too soon after they are laid. Allow a longer time for boiling a new-laid egg than for one that is three or four days old. Have ready a saucepan of boiling water; put the eggs into it gently with a spoon, letting the spoon touch the bottom of the saucepan before it is withdrawn. Boil for ten to fifteen minutes and then place in a basin of cold water for a few minutes. This will shrink the meat from the shell and make the egg easier to peel.

PRESERVED HENS EGGS

Here is a most effective way to preserve eggs, keeping them fresh from August until Spring. Take a piece of quick-lime as large as a good-sized lemon, and two teacupfuls of salt; put it into a large vessel and slack it with a gallon of boiling water. It will boil and bubble until thick as cream; when it is cold, pour off the top, which will be perfectly clear. Drain off this liquor, and pour it over your eggs; see that the liquor more than covers them. Store in a stone jar.

Another method: Pack the eggs in a jar with layers of salt between, the large end of the egg downward, with a thick layer of salt at the top. Cover tightly and store in a cool place.

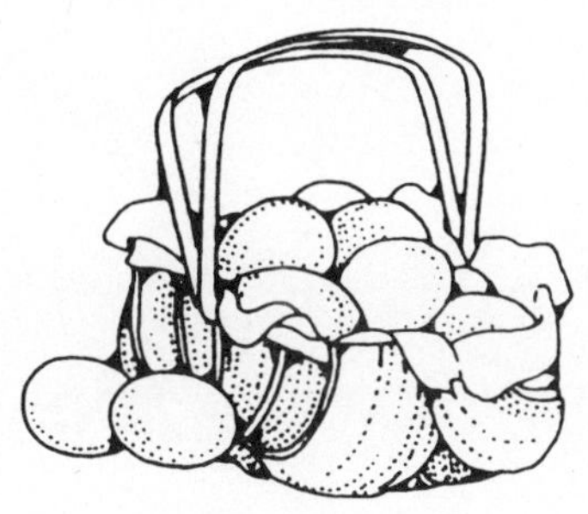

RICE GRIDDLE CAKES

Mix two cupfuls of cold boiled rice, one pint of flour, one teaspoonful of sugar, one half teaspoonful of salt, one and one-half teaspoonfuls of baking powder, one egg, a little more than half a pint of milk. Sift together the dry ingredients and then get rid of any lumps in the rice. Mix the rice with the beaten eggs and milk and add in the dry ingredients. Make this into a smooth batter. Drop in large dollops on a hot griddle and bake nicely brown. The cakes can be fairly large. Serve hot with syrup or honey.

GODEY'S LADIES MAGAZINE

Godey's Ladies' Magazine was inspired by French publications of the same type. Founded by Louis Antoine Godey in 1830 the publication dealt with fashion, food, health and literature, and was a trend-setter in every way. No doubt young Jane Wilkinson Long saw it on many occasions, although it was difficult to find in early Texas. Still, her Aunt Ann Wilkinson was a woman of style and grace. She likely sent Jane copies via the steamships or Jane ordered such publications from New Orleans which was already a thriving port of entry both for New York shipping and that of Europe.

GODEY'S MAGAZINE PIE

Ingredients include butter, sugar; flour, a pinch of salt to taste, one pint of heavy cream and a dollop of essence of vanilla.

Spread butter, softened, one-eighth inch thick in unbaked pie crust. The receipt is elsewhere in this book on page 49. Sift sugar one-eighth inch thick over butter. Sift flour one-eighth inch over sugar. Pinch of salt may be added to flour. Mix one-half teaspoon essence of vanilla into one pint heavy cream. Pour over all. Bake at 450 degrees in the hot part of the oven for ten minutes and then at 325 degrees 'til custard is set.

LONE STAR FRUIT CAKE

Ingredients:

2 cups fresh sweetmilk
1/2 cup loaf sugar
1 coffeecupful of sorghum
Teaspoonful of cinnamon
Teaspoonfu of cloves, crushed
Dash of nutmeg
2 teaspoons baking powder or small yeast cake
2 1/4 cupfuls flour
1/4 teaspoon salt
3 fresh eggs
Flavoring - can use rum or whiskey to taste
1 cup pecans; 1 cup raisins; 1\2 cup candied cherries if they can be had; 2 cups coconut

Begin by putting the spices into the sorghum and allowing it to sit aside for a time. Mix in your dry ingredients and set them aside as well. Next, stir the milk, sugar and eggs together. Add flavoring to this. Then add the molasses and spices and gradually beat in the flour until the batter is smooth. Put in the pecans, raisins, cherries and coconut. Bake three or four hours in a tolerably hot oven where the fire is steady. Use a broom straw to test the batter. When it is done, let it cool for several hours. This cake keeps best in a tight container where it can be kept for several months.

SAM HOUSTON COMES TO TEXAS

Mr. Sam Houston came to Texas from Tennessee under unusual circumstances. Some say he was sent by Andrew Jackson to put Texas in the pocket of the United States. He is an endlessly fascinating man and deserves careful study. He stayed at the Brazoria Inn. Some say he planned his military strategy there. He most certainly knew Jane. Whatever brought him to the state, he remained to fight for independence and led the rag-tag Texas army to victory at San Jacinto. Houston was elected the first President of the young nation, and later was governor. His allegiance to Texas was never doubted. Today there is a great city named for him, site of his first inauguration, and Sam Houston State University bears his name.

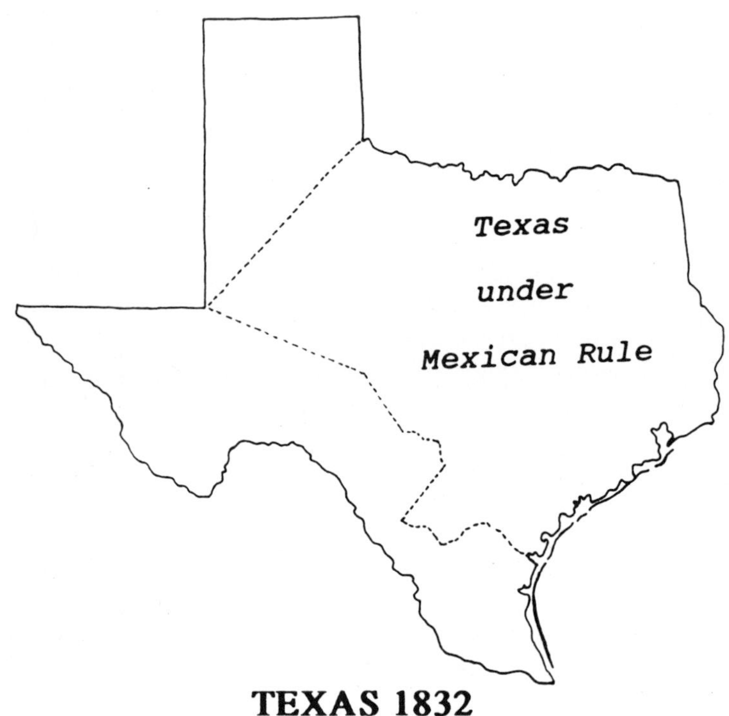

TEXAS 1832

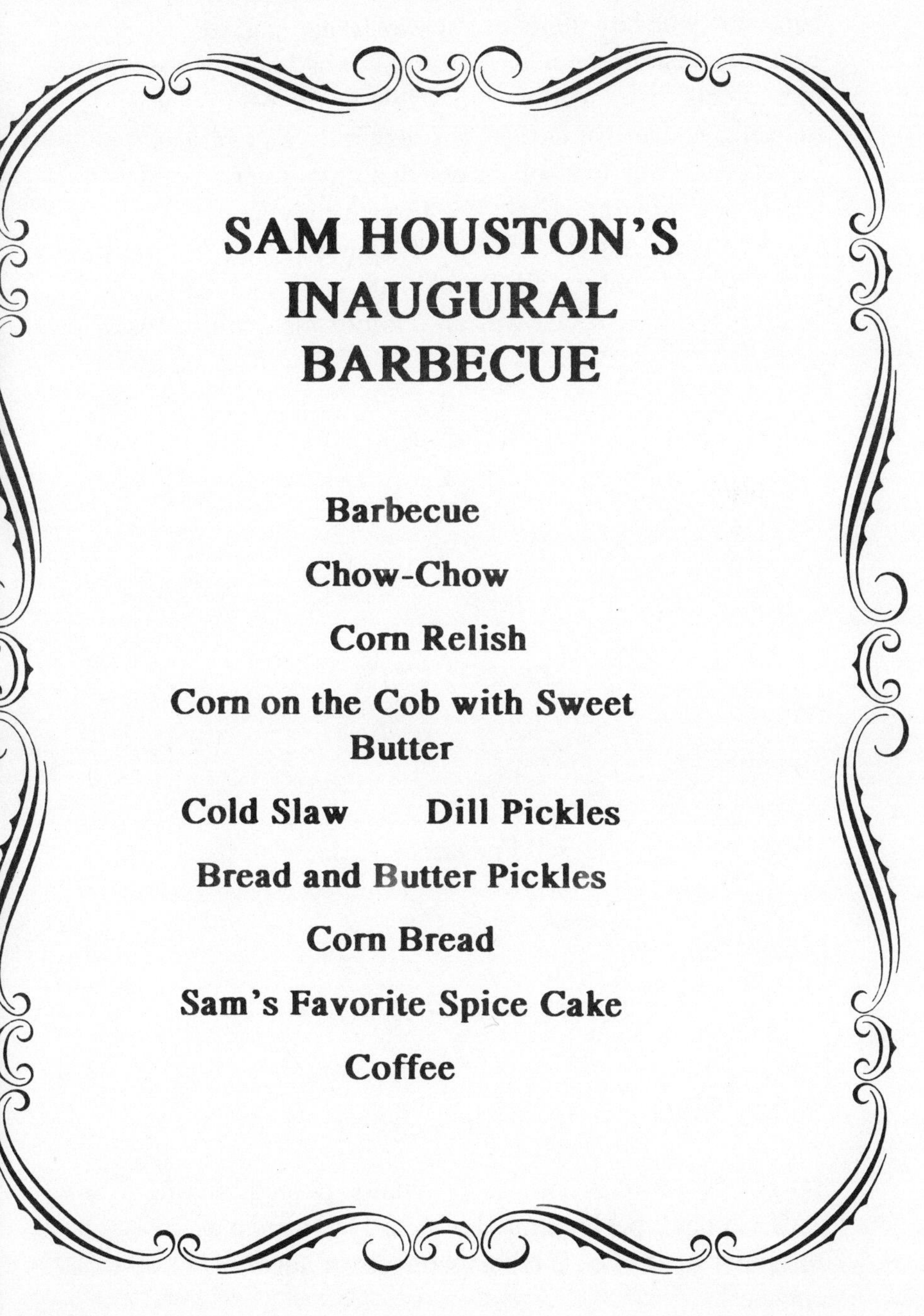

SAM HOUSTON'S INAUGURAL BARBECUE

Barbecue

Chow-Chow

Corn Relish

Corn on the Cob with Sweet Butter

Cold Slaw Dill Pickles

Bread and Butter Pickles

Corn Bread

Sam's Favorite Spice Cake

Coffee

ORIGINS OF BARBECUE

The main thing Jane's guests knew about Texas barbecue was how delicious it was to eat, and like everyone else in the new nation, Jane had her own secret ingredients that added a savory bite to the beef or pork or venison. One thing that was generally known was that to barbecue was to cook an entire animal over a solid bed of hot glowing coals. The French may have originated the practice, calling it "barbeagueve," which meant from snout to tail. Probably it had much earlier origins, but a barbecue was an outdoor meal which made it perfect for the trail.

BARBECUE

Ingredients:

Half a beeve; a pig, wild or tame; venison roasts; 1 whole kid(goat)

BARBECUE SAUCE

Ingredients:

3/4 cup butter or bacon fat; 6 tomatos pureed; 4 chili pods, cooked, peeled and chopped; Herbs such as coriander or thyme; 2 tablespoonfuls of sugar; 1/4 cup of vinegar

CHOW-CHOW

Ingredients:

1 gallon green tomatos; 1 cabbage, biggest you can pick; 8 large onions; 12 sweet peppers; one quarter pound of hot peppers; 1/3 cup of salt; 1 quart vinegar; 2 cups well water; 2 cups sugar

Chop tomatos, cabbage, onions and sweet and hot peppers fine as you can. Salt the entire mixture, but don't put in too much or you'll ruin it. Add the sugar, water and vinegar. Cook the vegetables in a heavy pan until tender which will not require a great deal of time. Everything will blanch out to a pale near white color. Put into a heavy stone crock and seal. Chow-chow is good with all kinds of game and will keep indefinitely.

CORN RELISH

Ingredients:

1 1/2 dozen ears of sweet corn ;1 head of cabbage; 4 large onions; sweet peppers; hot pepper such as jalapeno, about two; 2 quarts vinegar; 2 pounds sugar; 2 tablespoons mustard; 1 tablespoonful of turmeric, like ginger; 1/3 cup salt

Cut the corn off the cob and set aside. Chop the cabbage, onions, sweet and hot peppers and mix them with all other ingredients except for the corn. Cook for about thirty minutes and then add the corn while you cook the relish another fifteen to twenty minutes. While the relish is still hot, pour into a heavy crock and seal. This is excellent with barbecues, wild duck, venison and other game.

CORN ON THE COB

Gather the corn early in the morning and cook it on the same day you gather it for the best flavor. Strip off the husks and pick out all the silk. Put it in a tin pail of boiling hot water. If the corn is a day or more old, add a tablespoon of sugar to the boiling water, but NO SALT. Salt makes the corn tough. Boil twenty minutes fast and serve. Or you may scrape it or cut it from the cob, put in plenty of butter and a bit of salt, and serve in a covered vegetable dish. The corn is much sweeter when cooked with the husks on, but requires a longer time to boil.

Note: Corn left over makes a fine breakfast dish. Cut the corn from the cob and put it into a bowl with 1 cup of milk to every cup of corn. Add 1/2 cup of flour, 1 egg, a pinch of salt and a little butter. Mix well into a thick batter and fry in small cakes in very hot butter. Serve with plenty of butter and powdered sugar.

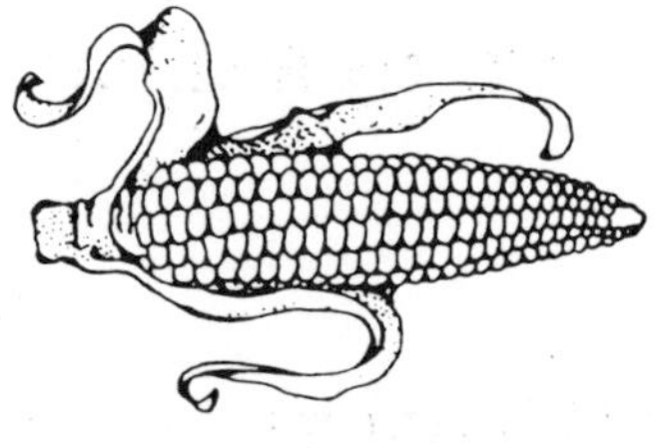

COLD SLAW

Select the finest head of bleached cabbage - that is to say one of the finest and most compact of the more delicate varieties: cut up enough into shreds to fill a large vegetable dish or salad bowl, that to be regulated by the size of the cabbage and the quantities required. Shave very fine and after that chop up the cabbage, the more thoroughly the better. Put this into a dish in which it is to be served after seasoning it well with salt and pepper. Turn over it a dressing made for cold slaw.

COLD SLAW DRESSING

Beat up two eggs with two tablespoonfuls of sugar. Add a piece of butter the size of an egg. A teaspoonful of mustard. A little pepper. And lastly, a teacup of vinegar. Put into a dish over the fire and cook like a soft custard. Some think it improved by adding half a cupful of thick sweet cream. In that case use less vinegar. Either way is very fine.

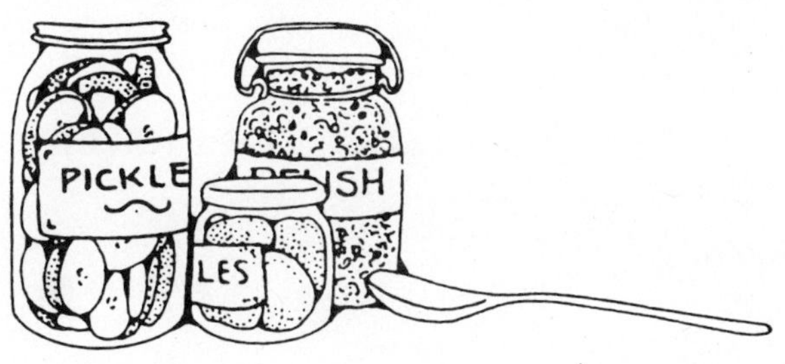

DILL PICKLES

Women are so proud of their dill pickle receipts it's hard to get one if there isn't one in the family already. This one is from Jane's Aunt Anne Wilkinson in Natchez, Mississippi, but no one knows its origins. She wouldn't say. Here it is.

Ingredients:

10 cups vinegar
20 cups well water
10 tablespoons of salt
Fresh dill to your taste
Pinch of cream of tartar
Grape leaves
Garlic pods
Sweet peppers

Pick cucumbers early in the morning for freshness. If you start with fresh cucumbers, your pickles will be crisp. Clean them thoroughly and set them into however many crocks you hope to fill. Put grape leaves under the cucumbers. Place stalks of dill in each crock along with garlic pods and sweet peppers. For hotter dills, add hot peppers to each crock. Boil your vinegar and water with the salt. Add a pinch of the cream of tartar. Pour the hot boiling water over the pickles until they are covered. Seal the crock and let stand for about two to three weeks for the best taste. As you can see, you might wish to add some other spices that are more to your liking, even onion.

BREAD AND BUTTER PICKLES

Ingredients:

12 cucumbers
6 onions, small
1/2 cup salt
2 cups of sugar
1 teaspoon ginger
1 teaspoonful cream of tartar
1/2 teaspoon black pepper
1 teaspoon cornstarch or flour
2 teaspoonfuls of mustard seed
2 cupfuls of vinegar

I needn't remind you to pick your cucumbers fresh the day of putting them up. Wash, peel and slice the cucumbers and onions. Let these stand in salt water about two hours. Bring sugar, flour or cornstarch, spices and vinegar to a boil for only a minute. Add the cucumbers and onions into the boiling water only until they are just cooked and still crisp. Next you put them into a crock and seal it. You should have nearly three pints of the pickles.

SAM HOUSTON'S GOLDEN SPICE CAKE

Ingredients:

7 egg yolks
1 whole egg
2 cups brown sugar
1 cup molasses
1 cup sweet butter
1 teacup sour milk

1 tsp. of soda
5 cupfuls of flour
1 tsp of ground cloves
2 teaspoons of ground cinnamon
2 teaspoons of ginger
1 nutmeg ground
A speck of cayenne pepper

Beat eggs, sugar and butter to a light batter before adding the molasses. Then add the molasses, flour, spices and milk. Beat it well together and bake in a moderate oven. If you use fruit, take two cupfuls of raisins, flour them well, and put them into the batter last.

Birthday Picnic

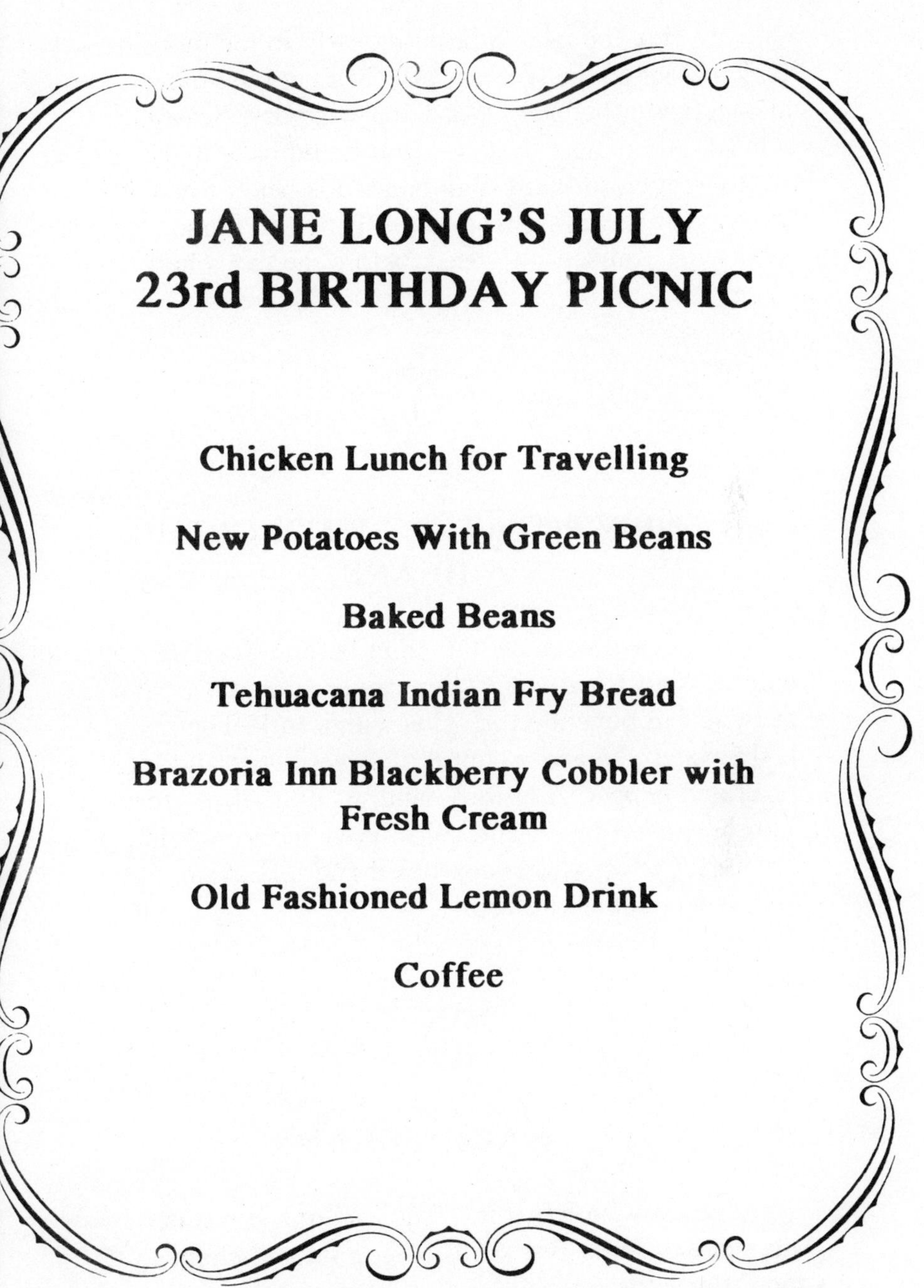

JANE LONG'S JULY 23rd BIRTHDAY PICNIC

Chicken Lunch for Travelling

New Potatoes With Green Beans

Baked Beans

Tehuacana Indian Fry Bread

Brazoria Inn Blackberry Cobbler with Fresh Cream

Old Fashioned Lemon Drink

Coffee

CHICKEN LUNCH FOR TRAVELLING

Wring the neck of a pullet early in the morning. Pluck and singe the feathers off, then cut the young chicken down the back. Wash and wipe dry. Season with salt and pepper. Use a drip pan and bake in a moderate oven for almost an hour. It is better to cook it this way for travelling than to put butter on it and thereby get yourself all greasy before the day's half begun.

NEW POTATOES WITH GREEN BEANS

Dig your potatoes the night before. Scrub them and boil them for about 30 minutes or so in a deep pot until you can puncture the skins with a fork. Then pour off the water and add a cupful of sweet butter and lots of salt and pepper. Add four handfuls of cooked green beans for added flavor and color. Pour the receipt into a large bowl, cover with a cup towel and take them with you. Delicious hot and cold.

BAKED BEANS

Begin with leftover "frijoles" or red beans. Add a cup of molasses, strips of hog fat and chunks of onion. Cook these for at least an hour and they can cool all night. Sticky and good. Easy to carry on a picnic.

TEHUACANA INDIAN FRY BREAD

Ingredients:

2 teacups flour
2 pinches baking powder or cream of tartar
1/2 tea cup cream
Pinch of salt
1 tablespoon lard cut into small bits, plus 1 pound for frying

Combine flour, baking powder and salt and sift into a deep china bowl. Add the bits of lard. With your fingertips rub the flour and fat together until the mixture favors flakes of coarse meal. Pour in milk and stir ingredients until the dough can be gathered up into a ball. Cover the bowl with a piece of muslin and let rest for two hours. After two hours, divide the dough into three equal pieces. On a board that's been dusted with flour, roll each piece into a circle about eight inches across and one-fourth of an inch thick. Cut two slits side by side through the dough, making the slits about the length of your hand, with one inch between each slit. In a sturdy skillet, melt lard over moderate heat until it is hot. Fry the breads one after the other for about two minutes on each side, turning them once. Be sure to use tongs or long forks when turning the bread. The bread should swell slightly and be crisp and brown like the color of pecan wood. Lay out on paper to drain and serve warm with honey.

BRAZORIA INN BLACKBERRY COBBLER WITH FRESH CREAM

Jane's boarders at the Inn asked her to make this whenever the blackberry bushes were heavy with fruit. This was a real delicacy mainly because the bushes bore fruit only in the summer months and pickers had to beat the rattlesnakes to the berries.

Ingredients:

2 quarts of fresh blackberries
1/2 teacup sugar
1 teacup sifted flour
1 teaspoon baking powder
Pinch of salt
1/2 teacup milk
1/2 teacup light syrup

First you sweeten your fruit and put in some cow's butter. Set over the fire until it comes to a rolling boil. While you are waiting, mix the other ingredients for your topping. Pour the boiling fruit mixture into your cobbler pan, put the topping over it and bake in the oven at 350 degrees for just over one-half an hour. Serve it with fresh cream and your guests just won't want to leave the table.

OLD FASHIONED LEMON DRINK

This is easy and everyone loves lemonade. Merely take a dozen lemons. For each half lemon, you add a tablespoon of white sugar, in this case 24. Then add 24 strawberries, two peaches cut fine, and two quarts of well water.

HARVEST SUPPER FOR HUNTERS

Squirrel Soup

Fried Rabbit

Jane's Texas Trail Chili

Buttermilk Biscuits

Dandelion Honey

Vinegar Pie

Bread Pudding

Coffee

SQUIRREL SOUP

Be sure you're feeding good hunters before you send out invitations. You'll need fifteen good sized squirrels. Once the game is skinned, wash and quarter the squirrels. If you can, get out any buckshot. Put the squirrels into a big stew pot more than half full of water, adding about three tablespoonfuls of salt, directly after breakfast. Cover the pot and set it over a low fire out of the way. Let it simmer and not boil. After a few hours have passed and other chores are done, then you add your vegetables. Corn, Irish potatoes, lima beans and if you have any, tomatos. Let these cook for about thirty to forty minutes, and then you may want to strain the soup through a coarse colander when the meat has boiled to shreds so as to get rid of the squirrel's troublesome little bones. Then return to the pot and boil a while longer. Melt butter and mix it with flour until it is smooth. Put this into the pot to thicken the soup. Pour the soup into a soup tureen and serve hot with biscuits and sweet butter.

FRIED RABBIT

The hunters could be trusted to provide fat autumn rabbits. Skin the rabbits and then wash them thoroughly and put into boiling water. Let the game boil for at least two minutes. Drain it and then allow it to cool. After that cut it into joints. Dip the pieces into beaten egg and flour seasoned with salt and pepper. When all are ready, fry the rabbit in hot fat over a moderate fire much as you would fried chicken. Once the rabbit is cooked, pour off most of the fat and add a spoonful of flour to the remaining fat. Turn in a cup of milk or cream and let all boil up. Turn this over the rabbit or over mashed potatoes. As good as chicken and some say better!

JANE'S CHILI

Ingredients:

Chili pods, mild and hot, crushed, about 2 tablespoons-ful
1 quart water
1 lb. beef suet, cut up
5 lbs. beef cut in chunks
3 pieces of fresh garlic, crushed
Comino
2 onions, sliced fine
4 tablespoons cornmeal for thickening
Flour
Water to thin the chili
Salt to taste

Use a dutch oven to make chili. Begin by boiling the chili pods until they are soft and you can remove the seeds and stems and pull off the skins which you don't want to use. The seeds are too hot, even for those who love heat in their food. Save the water you cooked the chili pods in. Chop up the chili pods and save. Put the suet into the bottom of the Dutch oven and put over the fire. This should be all right to cook the rest of the meat, but you can add some hog fat if you need to. Then put in the cut up meat and the garlic and cook until the meat is done. After that, add the comino and onions and cook until they are done too. Mix in a separate bowl the cornmeal, flour, salt and a little water, making a paste. Put in the chopped chili pods and mix this into the meat. Add at least a quart of water that you cooked the chili pods in, and during the time the chili is simmering, you'll add more water, but don't thin it out too much. Now some people do put in some other things, but the men at my table have complained they don't like tomatos in chili so I leave that out. Usually there is no chili left over, especially in cold weather. Corn bread goes well with it.

BUTTERMILK BISCUITS

Ingredients:

2 cups flour
4 teaspoon baking powder or a small yeast cake
4 tablespoons fat
2/3 cup of buttermilk

Mix the flour, the baking powder and salt. Cut in the fat with a knife. Continue to use the knife to slowly add in the buttermilk until a soft dough forms. Pat out the dough on a floured dough board until the dough is two-thirds of an inch thick. Take a biscuit cutter and cut out the shapes. Place the biscuits side by side in a heated skillet and bake in a moderate oven for about fifteen minutes. Serve hot with fresh butter.

DANDELION HONEY

Dandelion honey is always good. However, on the trail, should you encounter wild bee trees and if you have someone competent to rob them, you are likely to get some other kinds of honey, such as sweet clover honey, honeysuckle or even a mesquite flavored honey. These are all good, particularly if you gather the honeycomb. Some say that honey can keep down illnesses, and we know for certain that a little honey with lemon and whiskey is a Godsend against chills.

To extract honey from the honeycomb, first strain the comb through a sieve to free the honey from the wax. Melt it with gentle heat in a kettle over a low fire. Take off the scum with a skimmer or a large spoon as fast as it appears. Let cool and pour into crocks. Seal with cloth and wax so as to be airtight.

BEESWAX

The uses for beeswax would fill a book. The early pioneers used it in preparations for bed ticking, candles, cement, coloring, soaps, furniture and floor polish, lotion for chapped hands, waterproofing harnesses and leathers, sealing wax, making shoe strings, storing silks and packing woolen goods.

PIE CRUST

Ingredients for two crusts:

1 and 1/4 teacupful of lard
3 and 1/2 teacups of flour
1 teaspoon of salt
3/4 cupfuls of cold water

Mix lard and salt together and add in the flour. Cut these together until you have small pieces about the size of a blackeyed pea. Sprinkle cool water over the dry mixture and blend it in. Keep adding water until all the mixture is moist. Cover your fingers with flour and form the dough into a ball. Next you pour flour onto a hard surface and you roll out the ball of dough from the center until it is about one-eighth of an inch thick. It is easy to transfer the dough into your pie pans if you wrap it over the roller, or you can simply fold the dough in half and lift it gently into place.

VINEGAR PIE

Ingre-
dients:

1 egg
4 tablespoons vinegar
1 tablespoon of fresh lemon juice if it can be had
1 tablespoon flour
1 teacupful of sugar
1/4 teacupful of hot water
1 pie shell

Cook your pie shell a light brown and set it to cool. Mix your flour and sugar and add in boiling water. Cook this for five minutes or so, and then add in the egg which should be well beaten. Stir and cook for another minute or two. Add vinegar. If you have a lemon, you can add a tablespoon of fresh lemon juice, but as lemons are hard to come by, this may be omitted and add just a little extra vinegar, may be a teaspoonful. Pour all into the pie shell and set it in a cool place. Should set in time for supper.

BREAD PUDDING

Ingredients:

Take two-day old bread and crumble it in a large mixing bowl. Add about a quart of sweet milk and let that soak for a few minutes. Then add a cup of sugar, five eggs, a half cup of melted butter and essence of vanilla. Some like to add raisins or pecans if you have them. Mix these and turn them into a greased baking pan. Cover this and bake for at least 25 to 30 minutes. Once the pudding is set, you can add a little sugar on top. Add fresh cream for the best taste.

THE OLD 300'S FIRST THANKSGIVING AT SAN FELIPE DE AUSTIN

Wild Turkey

Corn Bread Stuffing with Oysters

Ladies' Cabbage

Mashed Potatoes

Greens

Ki's Autumn Pumpkin Bread

Sweet Potato Pie

Pecan Pralines

Brazoria Inn Peach Jam

Thanksgiving

WILD TURKEY

You may be lucky to shoot a young turkey, but you'll still need to get rid of the gamey taste and you can do this by soaking the plucked bird in sweet milk. First, however, you carefully remove the feathers and singe the stubble. Be careful not to break any of the internal organs. Remove the crop especially with care. Cut off the head and tie the neck close to the body by drawing the skin over it. Now rinse the inside of the turkey several times. Add some soda to the water and rinse it again to get rid of any sourness. Use a clean piece of muslin to dry the turkey and at this time you may want to soak the bird in the milk. Once this is done for a few hours and you have again rinsed out the bird, you stuff the inside with dressing. After this, sew up the turkey with a strong thread. Tie the legs and wings to the body. Rub soft butter over the entire bird and sprinkle a little salt and pepper. Place the turkey in a large pan and pour in a cup of hot, boiling water. Set the pan in the oven. Baste the turkey often, turning it occasionally for even cooking. Cooking for a long time over a medium fire will give you a tender delicate meat. You'll know it is done when you pierce it with a fork and the liquid runs out perfectly clear. If you see some part trying to burn, put butter on that place.

CORN BREAD STUFFING WITH OYSTERS

Back east where Jane was born the dressing or stuffing was made with light bread. In Texas, because corn meal was plentiful, dressing was made with it.

Ingredients are readily available and simple. Chop a half cup of onion. Use bacon grease from breakfast. Add in 2/3 teacup of butter and a receipt of corn bread from page 86. If they suit you, add fresh shucked oysters, cut up, and salt and pepper.

Melt the bacon grease and put in the chopped onion. Brown it and then add melted butter. Mix in the torn corn bread. Add salt and pepper. Add the cut up oysters and pour in stock from cooking the turkey giblets to keep the dressing moist. Bake in a moderate oven for about forty minutes.

CARROTS

Go to your storm cellar and fetch 20 carrots. Wash them and peel them, and slice lengthwise very thin. Drop into boiling salted water and let them cook until just tender. Pour out the water and add fresh butter about the size of a large egg. Stir 'til the carrots are coated. Salt and pepper to your liking. Turn out into a vegetable dish and serve hot.

LADIES' CABBAGE

Boil a firm white cabbage 15 minutes, then change the water for more from the boiling tea kettle. When the leaves are tender, drain and set aside until perfectly cool. Chop the cabbage fine. Beat up two eggs, a tablespoonful of butter, salt and pepper, and three tablespoonfuls of rich cream or milk. Stir all together, and bake in a buttered pudding dish until brown. Serve very hot. This dish resembles cauliflower and is very digestible and palatable.

NOTE: Cabbages are not injured by frost, but wither and wilt in a drying heat. They should be kept in a cool, dark, and moist place, but should not be kept in standing water.

Pack them in sawdust in large casks or packing cases. Take care to have a layer of sawdust several inches thick between the cabbages and the box. Put them in any outhouse and let them freeze. They will keep green and fresh all winter.

MASHED POTATOES

Ingredients:

6 medium sized potatoes
Cup of hot milk or better, fresh cream
2-3 tablespoonfuls of sweet butter
Salt and pepper to taste

Dig potatoes, as many as needed, out from the root cellar. Pare off the skins and lay the potatoes in cold water half an hour. Put them in a tin pail or sauce pan with a little salt, cover with water and boil them until done. Drain off the water and mash them fine with a potato masher. Have ready a piece of butter the size of an egg, melted in half a cup of boiling hot sweet milk, and a goodly pinch of salt. Mix it well with the mashed potatoes until they are light and moist. Do not pat them down or smooth them because that will cause them to be heavy.

GREENS

About a peck of greens are enough for a mess for a gathering of six folks. Almost any sort can be used. We've had the best of luck with dandelions, chicory, mustard or turnip greens. All greens should be carefully examined, and the tough ones thrown out. Thoroughly wash through several waters until they are entirely free from sand. Adding a handful of salt to each pan of water while washing the greens will free them of insects and worms.

When ready to boil the greens, put them into a large pot half full of boiling water, with a handful of salt, and boil them until the stalks are tender - anywhere from 5 to 20 minutes. Remember that over-long boiling wastes the tender nature of the leaves and lessens both the flavor and nourishment of the dish.

As soon as they are tender, drain them in a colander, chop them a little and return them to the fire.

Season them with salt, pepper, and butter. The greens should be served as soon as they are hot.

As I mentioned early on in this receipt, this serves 6 people, but could well serve 60. Just add a little more of everything in its measure.

KI'S AUTUMN PUMPKIN BREAD

Ingredients:

3 and 1/2 teacups wheat flour sifted four or five times
2 teaspoons cream of tartar
3 pinches of salt
A spec of cinnamon
A spec of nutmeg
1 cup of warmed lard
4 large hen's eggs
2/3 cups of water
2 cups pumpkin without the seeds
3 cups of sugar

Pick your pumpkins and let them sit on the verandah a week. Deep colored pumpkins are the best generally. Cut the pumpkin in half and remove the seeds. Slice it thickly and pare off the outside. Put the pieces into a large pot or sauce pan with a little water and allow it to boil gently until it is tender. Set the pot in a warm place, but do not allow the pumpkin meat to burn. Allow the pumpkin to dry out some. It will look dark and red when ready which requires at least a half day over a low fire. Remember that you can also do the same with squash. Some people prefer the taste of squash because its flavor is not so strong. When the pumpkin or squash is tender, then strain it and then it is ready for your receipt.

Cook in the warm side oven in the late afternoon when the coals are just right. May need to add kindling to the fire.

In a large pan, sift together your dry ingredients, including the sugar, flour, salt, cinnamon, nutmeg and cream of tartar. Mix this up. Then add the remaining lard, eggs, water, pumpkin and mix this until it is smooth. Use your heaviest bread pan. Grease it and coat it with flour.

Slide your pan into the oven and let it cook about one hour or longer. To see if it's done, take a clean broom splint and insert. If the straw comes out clean, then the bread is done. Cool it on the porch and then wrap the bread in clean muslin. It's always better the second day.

The best way to serve the pumpkin bread is to slice it real thin and add fresh butter.

SWEET POTATO PIE

Ingredients:

4-5 Sweet potatoes, cooked and mashed
1 cup sugar 1/2 cup flour
1/2 cup honey Pinch of salt
1 and 1/2 cupfuls of warm sweet milk,
or half sweet milk and half cream
1 teaspoon ground cinnamon
1/2 teaspoon ginger

Cut the sweet potatoes across instead of lengthways. That way you will eliminate the strings. Beat the eggs and sugar and honey, and add in the other dry ingredients including the sweet potatoes. Pour into a pastry shell and cook in an oven not too hot for about 30 minutes.

PECAN PRALINES

Jane first tasted pralines when she accompanied her husband Dr. James Long to New Orleans in 1821. Pralines were originally a French confection named for Marshall Cesar du Plessis-Praslin whose cook invented them. While in other places they are not always made with pecans, they are in Texas because the nut is so plentiful.

Ingredients:

1 pound dark brown sugar	Speck of salt
3/4 cup rich cream	1 tablespoon butter

1/2 pound of pecan halves (about 2 teacupfuls)

Take a heavy pan and mix together all ingredients save for the pecans. Cook over a low fire until the sugar dissolves, stirring faithfully. Now you add your pecans and add another stick of wood to the fire to get it hotter. Cook and stir until a soft ball forms in a teacup of water. Remove from fire immediately and let cool. Once your mixture begins to thicken, drop by spoonfuls onto a greased surface. If the candy begins to stick to the spoon too much add some boiling water from your tea kettle. Cool and serve.

BRAZORIA INN PEACH JAM

There is nothing better than these Texas peaches. Pare them and for each pound of fine, just ripe peaches, add in three-quarters of a pound of sugar. Put the peaches into a heavy pan and stir over the fire, trying not to break up the fruit too much. Simmer for a half hour and then put the jam into crocks with tight tops on them. We had heard that one of the German settlers cut writing paper in a circle bigger than the top of the container and smeared egg white on it as a glue. This she put over the top of the crock to seal it. Let the jam sit for a month and it will be delicious all year 'round on fresh biscuits or Sally Lunn bread.

CHRISTMAS AT THE BRAZORIA INN

CHRISTMAS EVE SUPPER

Gulf Coast Jambalaya

Old South Spoon Bread

Rice

Stewed Onions

Baked Winter Squash

Brandied Peaches

Spiced Raisins

Date Cookies

Stephen F. Austin's Favorite Pecan Pie

Angus McFarland's Scottish Short Bread

GULF COAST JAMBALAYA

Ingredients:

Piece of butter size of an egg
Teacupful of chopped onions
Teacupful of mild green peppers, chopped
Handful of leeks, chopped
Two cups of chicken broth
Two cupfuls of water
Salt and pepper
Dried tomatos
Garlic cloves, chopped
Four or five largest catfish. You can use bass or perch, and sunfish if that's all you can catch, but be sure and filet these for they have many small bones.
Crawdads, about 2 pounds with the heads pulled off
Sausages
Ground sassafras

Melt the butter in a heavy iron skillet. Add the onion, mild peppers, garlic and leeks and saute until the vegetables are nice and tender. Add in the chicken broth, the water and salt and pepper to your liking. Bring this to a boil and add in your dried tomatos. Put to the back of fire and let simmer for an hour while you're cleaning your fish. Add a little water now and then so it won't scorch. Wash the fish and filet it. Clean the crawdads. Slice up the sausage. Add all ingredients to the pot and cook for a good thirty minutes. Taste and add ground sassafras and more salt and pepper. This is a hearty dish, especially good served on rice.

OLD SOUTH SPOON BREAD

Ingredients:

1 cup white corn meal
2 tablespoonsful of butter
2 teaspoons of sugar refined
1 teaspoon of salt
3 cups of sweet milk
4 fresh eggs, separated

Mix the first five ingredients in a pan over a moderate fire, stirring constantly until the mixture is thick. Allow this to cool while you separate the four eggs. Beat the yolks until they are fluffy. Whip the egg whites until they form a stiff peak. Add the beaten yolks to the cornmeal mush mixture and then fold in the egg whites. Pour the mixture into a baking pan that is ungreased. This sets up best if you then set that pan into a shallow pan of water and cook in a moderate fire for about an hour or until the spoon bread is set and browned on top. Note: Spoon Bread loves sweet butter, so have plenty handy for guests.

STEWED ONIONS

Peel onions, cut off the ends, put them into cold water and into a stew pan, and let them scald for two minutes. Remove that water from fire and pour on cold water. Add salt and boil slowly till tender, which will be in thirty or forty minutes, according to their size. When done, pour off all the water. Add a teacupful of milk, a piece of butter the size of an egg, pepper and salt to taste, a tablespoonful of flour stirred to a cream; let all boil up once and serve in a vegetable dish, hot.

An excellent way to peel onions so as not to affect the eyes is to take a pan full of water and hold and peel them under the water. However it is awkward to manage the knife and onions in this way.

BAKED WINTER SQUASH

Cut open the squash, take out the seeds, and without paring cut it up into large pieces; put the pieces on tins or a dripping pan, place in a moderately hot oven, and bake about an hour. When done, peel and mash like mashed potatoes, or serve the pieces hot on a dish, to be eaten warm with butter like sweet potatoes.

DATE COOKIES

Filling: 2 cups dates cut up
3/4 cup of water
3/4 cup sugar
1/2 cup pecans

Dough: 1 cup shortening
2 cups brown sugar
2 fresh hen eggs
1/2 cup buttermilk
Essence of vanilla
3 and 1/2 cups sifted flour
Speck of baking powder
1/2 tsp cinnamon
1 teaspoonful each of salt and soda

Cook the date filling until it is thick.

Grease your baking griddle. Roll out dough. Spread date mixture on top and then add next layer of dough. Cook in a medium oven for about 12 to 15 minutes. Allow to cool before cutting.

STEPHEN F. AUSTIN'S FAVORITE PECAN PIE

Ingredients:

1/2 cup sugar
1 cup dark sorghum
3 tablespoons fresh cow's butter
3 fresh eggs
1 teaspoon essence of vanilla flavoring
Pinch of salt
1 cup fresh pecan halves
1 tablespoon flour
1 tablespoon sugar
1 pie crust that is unbaked

Stir the half cup of sugar and sorghum over a moderate fire until they boil. Stir in your butter. Meanwhile beat the eggs until whites and the yellows are blended. Pour the hot mixture over the eggs and stir. Add flavoring, salt and pecans. Now mix the flour and 1 tablespoon of sugar. Sprinkle this over the bottom of the unbaked pie crust. Pour the filling into the crust and cook in the oven which should be moderate. Cook about 45 minutes.

ANGUS MCFARLAND'S SCOTTISH SHORTBREAD

Ingredients are simple, most of a pound of cow's butter, a teacup light sugar, four teacups flour that's been sifted, salt and a dash of essence of vanilla. Cream together the butter and sugar. Add your salt and essence of vanilla. Add all but a handful of the flour a little bit at a time. Turn out on a clean scrubbed board that you have first sprinkled with that handful of flour. Work the dough well with your hands. Don't hurry or your shortbread will be wanting. Put in a pan and bake not long, 10 to 20 minutes. If the color is not light brown, you didn't bake it enough. Cut into squares or press out with a short bread mold. Serve or keep.

BRANDIED PEACHES

Boil a pound of sugar in a pint of water. Drop in a dozen peeled peaches. Once the peaches are tender, which you can tell by touching them with a sharp fork, lift them out with a slotted spoon and put them to dry out on the back porch in the sun. While the peaches are sunning, let the syrup keep boiling until it is thick and cooked way down. Allow the syrup to cool. Meanwhile, fill several crocks with the peaches, only half way full. Add a tablespoonful of sugar every now and then. Pour in syrup 'til half full and then add brandy until full. Seal the crocks and store in the storm cellar. This is good to have during the seasons when no fresh fruits are available such as January and February. I've found that this recipe also works for cherries, grapes, pears and plums.

SPICED RAISINS

Boil raisins in water until they're tender. Mix one pound sugar, one half pint good vinegar and a half pint water and boil for fifteen to twenty minutes to make a syrup. To the syrup you add cloves, cinnamon and nutmeg. Pour the spicy syrup over the raisins. Pour them into a crock and seal with parrafin-soaked muslin. These keep well and are good any time of year, especially with venison.

CHRISTMAS DAY DINNER

Roast Goose and Stuffing

Mashed Sweet Potatoes With Pecans

Cranberry Sauce

Olde Timey Corn Fritters

Brazoria Inn Wild Clover Honey

Barbara Calvit's Gingerbread

Texas Pecan Fudge

Molasses Candy

Brazoria Inn Christmas Cake

Egg Nogg

Coffee

PIONEER CHRISTMAS CELEBRATIONS

Christmas in early Texas was as joyous an occasion as anywhere the holy day is celebrated on earth. Many worshipped. Others rode down the rutted streets of the new towns shooting their pistols and whooping. Some gathered in family groups and read the familiar passages from St. Luke. The traditions were as varied as the people who came to the vast territory in search of a new life. But on Christmas Eve and Christmas Day, the usual activities came to a halt in honor of the birth of the Christ Child, an observation that continues unto this day.At the Brazoria Inn, the celebration was especially festive because of hardships Jane had suffered at Point Bolivar years before. There would be buffets of food for guests. Jane herself would play the piano and sing. Angus McFarland would bring his Scottish bagpipes. And the men would be asked to check their guns at the door!

ROAST GOOSE

The goose should be about seven to eight months old, still tender. The fatter, the juicer the meat. Separate out the giblets which you will cook separately and use later for the gravy.

STUFFING

Stuff with the following mixture: Three pints of breadcrumbs, half a cup of butter or part butter and part salt pork, one teaspoonful each of sage, black pepper and salt, one whole onion chopped. Do not stuff very full. You stitch the openings together to keep in the flavor. Place in a large roaster with a heavy lid. Put in some water in the pan. Baste throughout the day with water and salt, and some may add vinegar. Turn the bird often for even browning. Bake about two hours. Once the bird is done, take it from the pan and spoon off the fat. You'll have a brown gravy left. Add the chopped giblets which you'll want to stew until they're tender. Thicken the gravy with flour and butter and bring this to a boil to serve over the corn bread dressing.

MASHED SWEET POTATOES WITH PECANS

Bake 8 to 10 sweet potatoes. When they are done, peel and mash them. Add a half cup of sugar, fresh butter and a little sorghum syrup. Put in half a cup of pecans. Then bake for about half an hour real slow. Good hot and cold.

CRANBERRY SAUCE

Take whole fresh cranberries and rinse and drain them. Sort them out until you have about 2 quarts worth. Put them in a heavy iron pot. Add three cups of water. Cook until all the berries pop. Add the sugar and boil for at least 20 minutes without a cover, stirring frequently to prevent sticking. The sugar will thicken the mixture and make a nice syrup. Turn out into a pretty glass bowl and allow to cool. Not only is this tasty, but it makes your Christmas table bright and pretty.

OLDE TIMEY CORN FRITTERS

Ingredients:

1 egg 1 and 1/2 teacups of sweet milk
1 and 1/2 tablespoons sweet butter, melted
2 teacups of flour
1/2 teaspoon baking powder or cream of tartar
1 teaspoon of salt 1 and 1/2 teaspoons sugar
Two cups of corn freshly cut off the ears. 4-5 ears.
Lard

Mix the dry ingredients all together and set them at hand. Beat the egg and add the milk and butter. Blend into the egg mixture. Mix in the cut corn and let the concoction set in a cool place. It will have a thickness that causes it to stick together when you drop it into deep hot fat and fry it. Drain on brown paper and then serve with Texas Wild Clover Honey.

BRAZORIA INN WILD CLOVER HONEY

Jane kept bees in later years and sold crocks of the honey to local buyers. Wild clover was plentiful in the area and made for an especially sweet-flavored honey.

BARBARA CALVIT'S GINGERBREAD

Barbara liked this recipe because her girls could help her make it and it kept well for company.

Ingredients:

2 fresh eggs — 3/4 cup of heavy sorghum syrup
1/2 cup fat — 3/4 cup brown sugar
2 and 1/2 cups flour
2 teaspoons cream of tartar
1 and 1/2 teaspoons ground cinnamon
1 teaspoonful ginger
1/2 teaspoon nutmeg
1/2 teaspoon cloves
1 cup boiling hot water

Add the eggs to the sugar, the sorghum and the melted fat. Add the dry ingredients. Last you pour in the boiling water. Pour into an iron baking pan and bake for about forty minutes. Test with a dry, clean broom straw. If it comes out dry, then the gingerbread is done. Add a little sweet cream butter to the gingerbread for a richer taste.

TEXAS PECAN FUDGE

Ingredients are 3 cups sugar, 1 cup milk ,1/2 cup pecans, a heaping tablespoonful of grated cocoa and 1 tablespoon sweet butter. Add essence of vanilla.

Combine sugar, cocoa, milk and butter. Cook over a low fire stirring constantly. When the candy begins to thicken, put a little bit into the cold water. If it forms a soft ball remove the candy from the fire. Add the essence of vanilla. Then beat the candy very hard, until creamy but not dry. Fold in your pecans and swiftly turn out into a buttered pan. When the candy sets, cut it into squares.

MOLASSES CANDY

Ingredients are at hand in most kitchens and include 2 cups of molasses, 1/2 teaspoon cream of tartar 1 teaspoon vinegar. Pour molasses into a heavy pan and boil for 20 minutes. Don't let it scorch. Add in the soda and boil for another quarter of an hour. Now and then drop a speck of the candy into cold water to see if it is brittle. Just before taking from the fire stir in a teaspoon of vinegar and beat. Turn out onto a heavy buttered platter. Cool and break apart into bite size pieces.

BRAZORIA INN CHRISTMAS CAKE

Ingredients:

1 lb. of this year's fresh shelled pecans
1/2 lb. candied pineapple from John Austin's store

1/2 lb. candied cherries	1 lb. dates
1 cup sugar	1 cup flour
Speck of baking powder	1/2 teaspoon salt
1 tsp nutmeg	1 tsp essence of
vanilla	4 fresh hen eggs

Simple to make. You mix all the ingredients together. Pour into a heavy iron baking pan lined with brown paper. Bake 2 hours in a slow oven. This is a cake that will keep well through the winter, but you probably won't have a bite left after your guests go home.

EGG NOGG

Separate out 8 egg yolks and beat them thoroughly. Then add two quarts of sweet milk. The secret is in what you flavor the egg nogg with. Vanilla flavoring is good, and on cold winter nights, you can lace the egg nogg with fine rum, brandy or Scotch whiskey, though not too much.

AUSTIN, FATHER OF TEXAS

Stephen Fuller Austin is called the Father of Texas. He was from Missouri, educated at Transylvania College in Lexington, Kentucky. Later he read law in New Orleans. When his father Moses died after gaining permission from the Spanish government to settle in Texas and bring in other settlers, Stephen took over his father's work. At the time, there were fewer than 8,000 permanent residents in Texas, and a number of Indian tribes whose numbers are not known because they were nomadic. He took the title of "empresario" and with the blessings of the ruling government successfully brought settlers into Texas. He was a peaceful man who loved learning, geography, farming and the country life. He was one of the last to join in the fight for independence against a young Mexican government that was in turmoil itself. It was only after Austin was imprisoned without right of trial or representation for eighteen months that he became a rebel and joined the fight for Texas' independence.

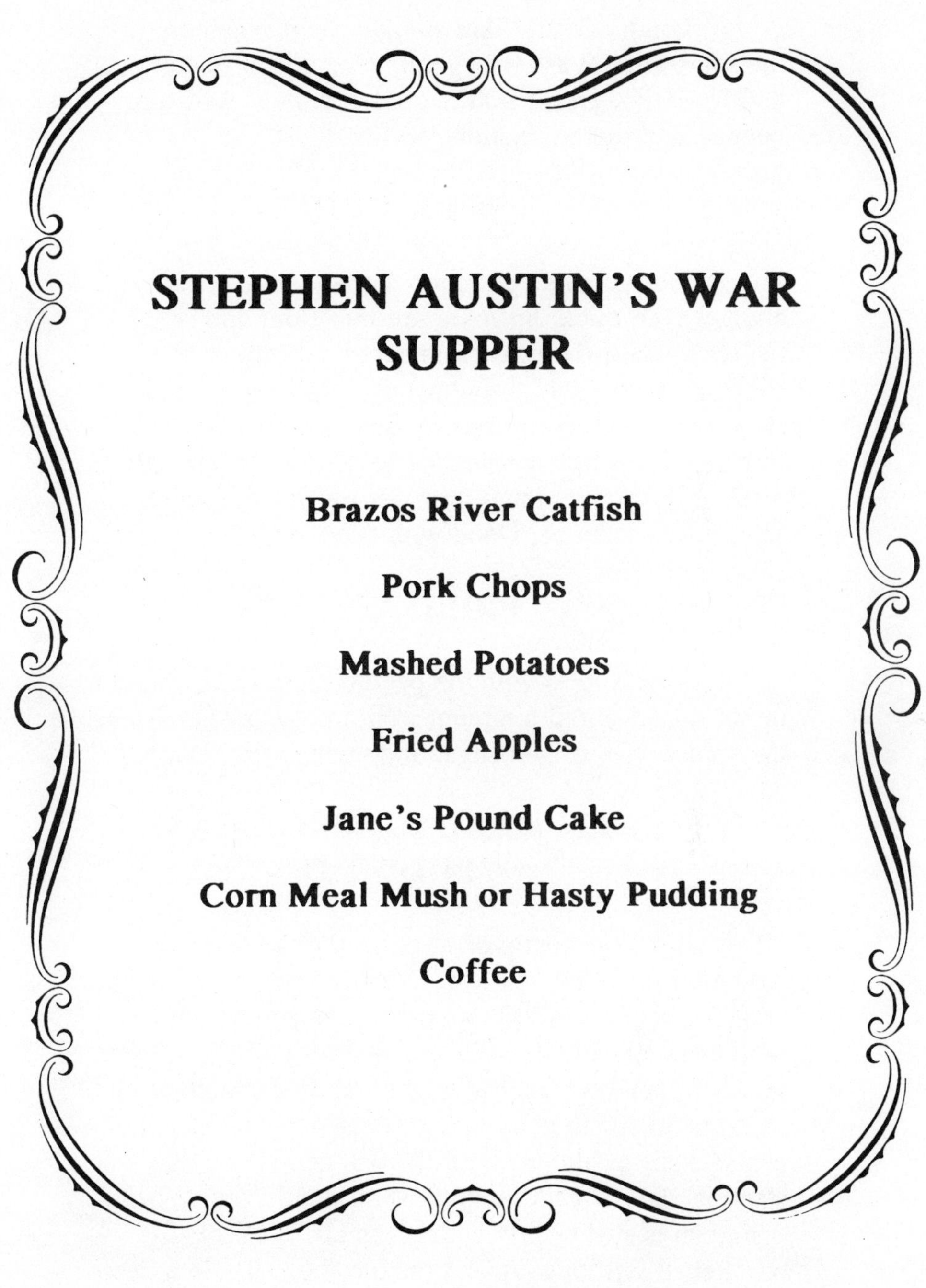

STEPHEN AUSTIN'S WAR SUPPER

Brazos River Catfish

Pork Chops

Mashed Potatoes

Fried Apples

Jane's Pound Cake

Corn Meal Mush or Hasty Pudding

Coffee

FRIED BRAZOS RIVER CATFISH

Catch catfish. Skin and gut them. Then cut off the sharp fins. Wash in several waters. Roll in cornmeal and fry in hot grease until a golden brown. Add salt, pepper, and there is nothing better.

PORK CHOPS

Plan on one pork chop per person. Cut chops about 1 inch thick. Sprinkle salt into flour and cover the chops with flour. Then in bacon fat, brown the chops on both sides. Some people like them plain fried. However, you can just brown them and then put them into a skillet with an onion, peppercorns and enough water to just cover them. Simmer for an hour and they are tender as can be. Good with fried apples.

FRIED APPLES

Slice apples with the peelings still on. Fry them in hot grease and drain them well on brown paper. Dust the apples with brown sugar and nutmeg or cinnamon.

CORN MEAL MUSH OR HASTY PUDDING

Boil two quarts of water in a clean stew pot. Add a tablespoonful of salt. Use sweet fresh yellow or white corn meal. Add it a handful at a time to the boiling water, all the while stirring with a long wooden spoon. When one handful is gone, then get another and continue to stir in the meal until it is as thick as you can still stir easily. Or until the wooden spoon will stand it . Stir a while longer over a gentle fire. When the mush is sufficiently cooked, in about twenty minutes, it will puff up and bubble. Turn it into a deep basin. It can be served hot with butter or cold with milk. You can add molasses or sugar. You can eat it like potatoes with meat and gravy. You can also use it to fry for breakfast.

JANE'S POUND CAKE

Ingredients:

1 pound sugar
1 pound fresh cream butter
5 fresh hen's eggs
1 pound wheat flour, sifted
1/2 cup of sweet milk
Pinch of salt

Cream your sugar and fresh butter until your arm is tired and then switch to the other side and keep on until the mixture is smooth. Then you add the eggs one at a time, beating them in before you add the next. Add in the milk and the flour, alternating one and then the other. Add the salt and pour the batter into a heavy cake pan. You cook the cake in a slow oven around one hour. Let the cake cool a bit and then turn upside down on clean cloth. The cake is best served with fresh butter and is truly a "pound" cake. For a little different taste, try fresh buttermilk in place of the sweet milk.

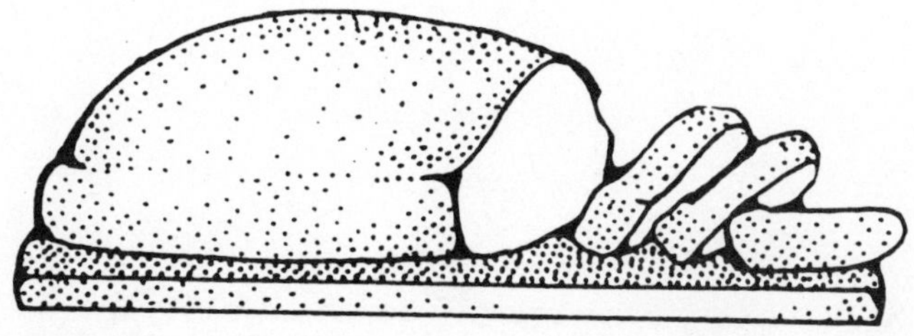

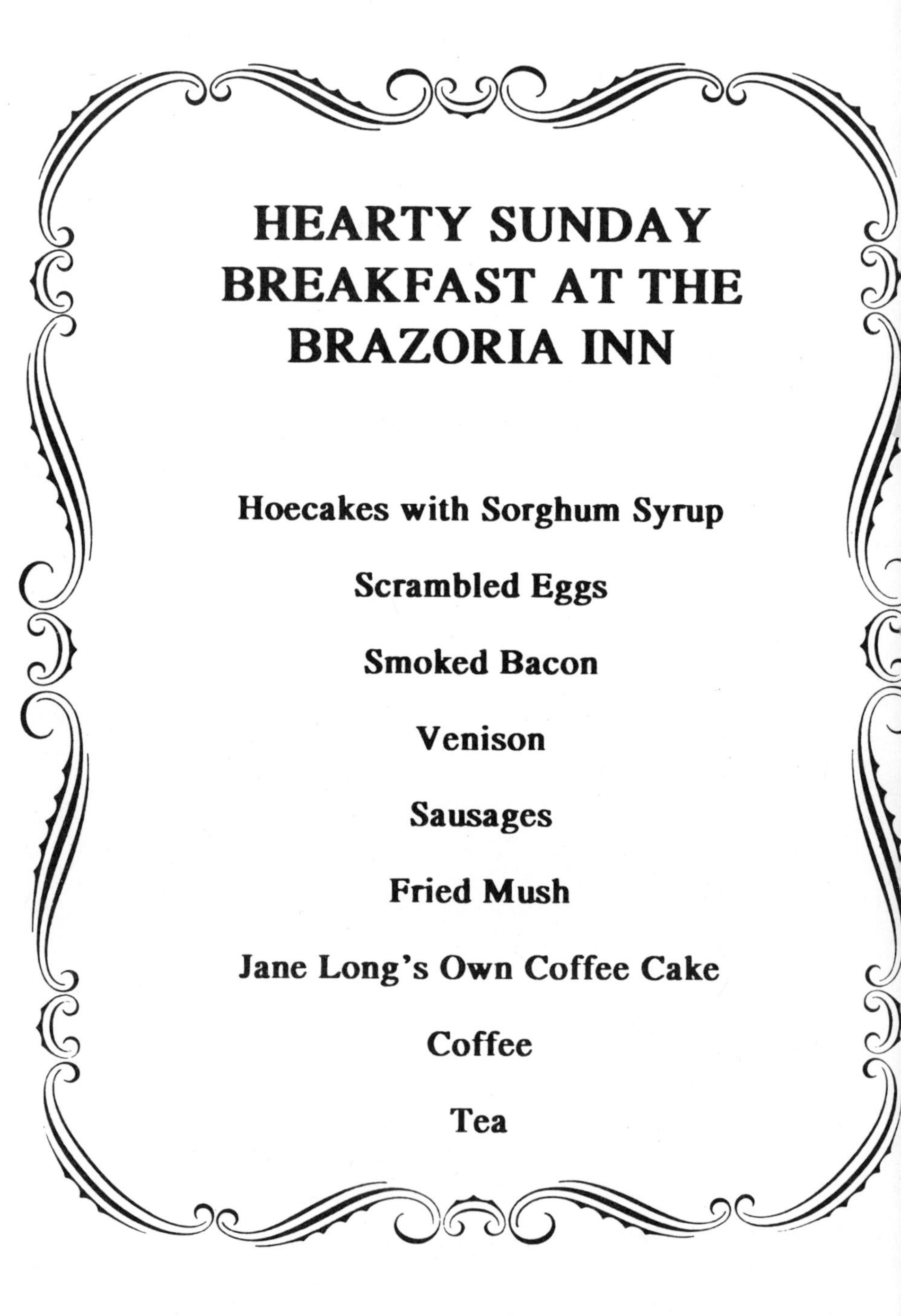

HEARTY SUNDAY BREAKFAST AT THE BRAZORIA INN

Hoecakes with Sorghum Syrup

Scrambled Eggs

Smoked Bacon

Venison

Sausages

Fried Mush

Jane Long's Own Coffee Cake

Coffee

Tea

HOECAKES

Ingredients:

3 cups cornmeal	1/2 cup hot boiling water
1 and 1/2 cups flour	5 fresh hen eggs
Cup or so of sour milk	Cream of tartar

Three cups sifted cornmeal should be scalded with hot water and then add a cup and a half of flour and a teaspoonful of salt. Mix in five fresh eggs well-beaten. This mixture will be thick and you need to add some sour milk to thin it down so you can bake it on a hot griddle. If you have soda, dissolve it in the milk and add it to the mixture. If you use sweet milk, put in baking powder instead of the soda, two large teaspoonfuls. These bake in a minute and fill people up for the entire morning, especially on cold days.

SORGHUM SYRUP

Sugar or sorghum cane, a cereal grass with broad cornlike leaves and a tall, pithy stalk, was one of Texas' first important exports, but before the farmers sent the valuable commodity away, they made certain that they had their own supply of sorghum syrup and sugar for the cold wet winters of the southeastern Texas coast areas. Once the cane was mature, the leaves were stripped and the cane cut, a backbreaking job that required stamina and strength. Next, the juice was extracted from the stalks by a crude sorghum mill and strained several times to get rid of debris from the stalks. Next the juice was cooked over a hot wood fire. The impurities still in the juice were skimmed out until the liquid was very clear, a process that required hours of careful work. Again, the cane syrup was strained through cheesecloth or muslin and poured into clean heavy crocks and sealed.

SCRAMBLED EGGS

Whip eggs light as you can. Add a little fresh cow's cream and salt and pepper. Be sure the skillet is hot as can be and pour the eggs in. Let them set up for maybe a half a minute or so, and keep on beating them with a fork. Should come out light and fluffy.

JANE LONG'S OWN COFFEE CAKE

Ingredients:

2 teacupfuls of brown sugar
2 teacupfuls of sweet cream butter
4 fresh eggs
1 cup of sorghum syrup or honey
2 teacupfuls of strong cold coffee
2 teaspoonfuls of soda
2 teaspoonfuls each of cinnamon of grated cloves
1 and 1/2 teacupfuls each of raisins and chopped pecans
10 cups of sifted flour

First, grease a heavy loaf pan. Then mix the sugar, butter and eggs until creamy. Mix in the sorghum or honey until the mixture is smooth. Add the coffee, soda and spices. Next, flour the raisins and pecans and mix them in as well. Bake the coffee cake for about one hour over a moderate fire.

FRIED MUSH

Prepare mush as in the receipt for Corn Meal Mush or Hasty Pudding found elsewhere in the book. Pack left over mush solidly in a wet bread pan. Set down in the well to cool. When cool turn out on a board and cut in 3\4 inch slices. Dip the slices in egg and flour and fry in deep fat until golden brown on both sides. Good with crisp bacon.

EASTER DINNER IN OLD TEXAS

Lamb Stew

Roast Wild Duck

New Potatoes with Parsley

Beet and Cabbage Slaw

Ann's Favorite Custard

Syrup Pie

Brazoria Inn Blackberry Preserves

Sally Lunn Bread

Coffee

LAMB STEW

Once the dressed lamb is brought into the kitchen and washed in several waters, cut it into small pieces about two inches square after you remove the fat. Put it in a deep iron pot with enough water to cover it and hang it over a medium hot fire. Let the lamb stew gently until it is partly done at which time you add a few thin slices of salt pork, two or three onions chopped fine, and three or four raw potatoes cut up into one-inch pieces. Add in about two potatoes and a half onion for each additional person you are feeding. Salt and pepper the stew to your taste. Continue gently stewing until the meat is tender. To make the stew go farther, you can drop in dumplings made like short biscuits and cut very small. Cook these about fifteen minutes longer. Thicken the gravy with a little milk and flour and serve.

ROAST WILD DUCK

A special note about roasting duck. You must give yourself plenty of time, else you might find hungry guests waitin' while the duck gets done. Wild duck should be hung out on the porch for several days before dressing, if the weather is cool enough. Pick, draw, clean thoroughly in several waters and wipe dry. Cut the neck close to the back. Beat the breast bone flat with a rolling pin and tie the wings and legs securely. Bake over a hot fire, letting the duck remain a few minutes at first without basting to keep in the juices. Then baste with melted butter and hot water. You have to be careful with wild duck. Overcooking ruins the flavor, but an underdone duck is not fit to eat. You may cook it anywhere from 45 minutes to 2 hours, but you must watch it carefully. Serve hot.

BEET AND CABBAGE SLAW

Chop cabbage fine. Slice beets in thin strips and mix together. A dressing of vinegar and sugar adds a fine flavor. Keeps well in a cool crock.

SALLY LUNN BREAD

Some said that Sally Lunn was from Bath, England, which claims to be the home of this wonderful bread. Others, however, said that a young woman selling the bread from morn 'til night on the streets of Bath called it "soleil et lune" which sounded like "Sally Lunn." In any case, everyone loved it. The excellent sweetish tasting bread, whose receipt was often used in the first Thirteen Colonies, became famous. This receipt makes two loaves. Usually Jane made at least eight for her boarders.

Ingredients are basic, 1 cup of sweet milk, 1/2 cup of lard, about a half teacupful of water, 4 cups sifted flour, about 1/3 cup of sugar grated, 2 teaspoons of salt, active dry yeast and 3 hen eggs.

Heat the milk, lard and water, though the lard does not have to melt all the way. Take your dry ingredients, but only about 1 and 1/2 cups of the flour, and mix them in with yeast and then you add your warmed liquids. Beat these together until they are well mixed. Add most of the remainder of the flour and the eggs and beat the entire mixture. Finally add the leftover flour. Mix this in. The batter should be thick. Cover your dough with a clean towel and let it rise for about 2 hours, 'til. double in size. You push down the dough and divide it into your pans. Again you leave it to rise in a warm dry place until it is about twice its size. Grease bread pans or skillet and let them sit near the fire while you prepare the loaves. Once it is ready, the fire should be even. Bake the bread for about 45 minutes and let it cool. This is a slightly sweet bread that is good with every meal. Be sure and have plenty on hand for folks always ask for second helpings!

ANN'S FAVORITE CUSTARD

A favorite of young Ann Wilkinson Long.

Ingredients:

3 hen's eggs
5 tablespoons light sugar
1 pint fresh milk
Pinch of salt
1 teaspoon essence of vanilla

First heat the milk over a fire. Break eggs into a china bowl. Add salt to the hen's eggs and beat. Stir it into the milk and pour into a dish strong enough to stand the heat of baking. Put this into a pan of water and bake at 325 degrees for one-half to three-quarters of an hour or until it feels firm to the touch.

BRAZORIA INN BLACKBERRY PRESERVES

Blackberries are plentiful in the Texas forests and byways. Pick a bushel of them, being very careful for they are so tasty they attract the vile rattlesnake that has been the death of some of our early settlers. Wash the berries over and over. Judge the weight of the fruit and plan for one pound of loaf sugar for every pound of the delicious fruit. Put the clean berries and the sugar into a heavy iron pot and cook over a low fire, slowly bringing it to a boil. Get the berries out first and put them into the waiting crocks. Allow the juice to boil a few minutes longer and then fill up the crocks with the delicious blackberry juice. Seal the crocks and store in a cool dry place. If you follow the process carefully and use clean containers, the fruit will keep for several years.

SYRUP PIE

Ingredients for two pies:

5 eggs — 3 cups sorghum syrup
Teacupful of butter — Pinch of salt
Essence of vanilla extra, about a tablespoonful
Sprinkle of nutmegPie crust receipt is on page 49

Bring the syrup to a boil and remove it from the fire. Right away, add the butter and the salt. Mix them in and cool the syrup. Beat the eggs and add in the essence of vanilla. Mix these with the syrup. Pour into pie crusts. Sprinkle the nutmeg over the top and cook pies in a moderate oven for about 45 minutes. You can use this same base receipt for a good pecan pie too.

KIAMATIA, LOYAL COMPANION

When Jane Wilkinson first came to live with her guardians, General James Wilkinson and his wife Ann in Natchez, before Mississippi was a state, she was given a young slave girl by Alabama cousins. Jane was twelve and Kiamatia was eight. Both were orphaned. They did not know it then but they would form a lifelong bond and apparent friendship that would last until Kiamatia's death in the 1860s.

A young and impetuous Jane followed Dr. James Long to Texas, and Kiamatia accompanied her. In fact, she saved Jane's life on the trail to Texas by giving her herbal teas to fight a devastating fever. Later, when the pair and young Ann Long were abandoned at Las Casas at Point Bolivar, Kiamatia helped Jane deliver her third child. Jane pulled Kiamatia through a terrible sickness that same winter. Together they survived the wilderness that was Texas.

Later, Kiamatia ran the kitchen at the Brazoria Inn and was known for her excellent "receipts" for biscuits, pumpkin bread, spring chicken and other fine victuals. The pair doctored many who had cholera and were among the first to teach how to prevent the disease. Later Jane opened the Verandah Inn in Richmond, and Kiamatia was at her side. At some point Kiamatia married and had a family, but those records are apparently lost. She worked for Jane Long until she died in the 1860s. Her descendants live in the area of Richmond, Texas, today.

In looking back, we realize that a slave had little choice where she went and thus Kiamatia went with Jane. At one point, a creditor tried to take Kiamatia from Jane for a debt her adventurer husband had made. Jane fought to get Kiamatia back. They were never again separated. Their story is one of loyalty, love and adventure. Both helped shape and civilize the nation of Texas, born out of a a vast promising wilderness.

A TRADITIONAL TEXAS COUNTRY DINNER

Texas Fried Chicken

Beef Steak

Corn Bread

Blackeyed Peas

Suet Pudding

Apple Fritters

Coffee

TEXAS FRIED CHICKEN

Salt and pepper are mixed into a double handful of flour. Roll cut up chicken in flour. Sizzle in hot lard 'til golden brown. Serve hot with mashed potatoes, fresh green beans, sliced tomatos and cucumbers.

BEEF STEAK

Take from the ribs or sirloin and remove the bone. Put butter or grease drippings into the frying pan and set it over a good hot fire. When it is hot, lay in the steaks. When cooked quite enough, that is browned but not cooked through, season with salt and pepper, turn and brown on the other side.

BLACKEYED PEAS

If you have saved your blackeyed peas from the summer, then take about a pound of them and wash through several waters. Fill up a heavy cooking pot with half water and put in the blackeyed peas, along with a slab of fat back. A large onion peeled should be added. Cook this together. Now if you are cooking fresh peas, add in some snap beans about half way through the cooking.

CORN BREAD

Grease your skillet and set it into a hot oven. Allow it to get very hot. Mix a double handful of cornmeal with about a half cup of water or more 'til it is very thin. Add then three eggs, one tablespoon of fat, a tablespoon of butter, about a teaspoon of yeast and a pinch of salt. Pour batter into the hot skillet and cook it in a hot oven. Serve with sweet butter. When corn bread is cold, it is good crumbled into a glass of fresh buttermilk.

SUET PUDDING

Ingredients:

1 and 1/2 cups chopped up suet
2 cups raisins
2 cups sweet milk
1 cup molasses
1/2 cup sugar
3 and 1/2 cupfuls of flour
1 teaspoon each cream of tartar, cinnamon, cloves ground up, nutmeg.

Mix these ingredients all together and steam them for three hours. Good with a sauce of half a cup of butter, 1 cup of sugar, molasses, raisins and pecans beaten thoroughly.

APPLE FRITTERS

If you are lucky enough to have some apples left over from the winter, then peel, core and slice them. Mix vinegar, sugar and nutmeg and soak the apples for the morning. Using four eggs and a cup of milk plus a handful of flour, make a nice thin batter. This can sit out awhile. In the afternoon near supper, melt a cup of butter in a fry pan and dip your apple slices into the batter. Then drop them into the pan over a good hot fire. Let them brown. Drain them and then sift pounded sugar over them. If you like nutmeg or cinnamon that adds a fine taste sprinkled over the hot fritters.

CHURNING BUTTER THE OLD-FASHIONED WAY

You must thoroughly scald the churn and then cool it with well water. Next you pour in the thick cream and churn fast at first. As the butter forms, you may slow your churning down a bit but keep your rhythm regular. In warmer weather, pour cool well water into the churn if the butter forms slowly. In winter, if the cream is too cold, add just a little warm water to bring it to the proper temperature. When the butter is formed, rinse the sides of the churn down with cool water and take the butter up with the wooden ladle, turning it just below the surface of the buttermilk so that you catch every stray bit of the precious commodity. You need a deep wooden tray in which you pour cold water. Into this plunge the ladle when you draw it from the churn. The butter will float off, leaving the wooden ladle free.

Next you collect all the butter with a wooden ladle, allowing the water to drain off. Squeeze and press the butter with the ladle. Then pour on more cold water and work the butter with the ladle to get the milk out. Drain off this water as well, and sprinkle a little salt over the butter, not quite a tablespoonful to a pound. Work the salt in a little and set the butter in a cool place for an hour to set up. Again, work the butter and knead it until not another drop of water is in it. The butter ought to be perfectly smooth and close in texture and polish.

With the ladle make up into rolls, little balls, stamped pats or however you wish to serve it.

The churn and wooden dasher, the tray and wooden ladle should be well scalded again so that the butter will not stick to them the next time you use them.

When you skim cream into your cream crock, stir it well into what is already there so that it may all sour alike. Do not add fresh cream to this within twelve hours before churning or the butter will not form quickly or perhaps not at all.

Butter was indispensable in almost all the food preparations. It helped in digestion and was far superior to the bear grease some of the households were using. The value of dairy cattle to the frontier way of life cannot be overstated. When Jane Long at last received her headright of land at Fort Bend, the first thing she thought of was acquiring a milk cow. Her good friend Stephen Fuller Austin carved a small cow from wood and promised to help Jane get a cow. He did so with the help of his sister Emily Perry who had brought her family to live in Texas. Without the cow, life in early Texas would have been much more difficult.

NATIVE TEXAS FRUITS -

PECANS, PERSIMMONS AND PUMPKINS BIG AS A MAN'S HEAD

Mary Austin Holley, cousin to Stephen Austin and one of the first journalists to describe Texas, wrote: "The grape abounds here in great variety and of the finest flavor, and no country can be better adapted to the culture of the vine than this." She went on to describe the successful manufacture of wine from native grapes as well as grape juice, jellies and preserves.

"Olives, oranges, lemons, figs, prunes and peaches" were available. Melons, pumpkins and cantaloupe could be easily grown. In particular it made sense to plant the pumpkins with the corn as the two were congenial. Stephen Austin had called Texas a virtual "Eden." Horticulturally, he was correct. Concerning man's behavior, he was on the money as well.

Beans, peas, sweet and Irish potatoes all were grown from seed in the early years of Anglo immigration to Texas. Mrs. Holley described a "paradise of pumpkins." They had to be planted only once. "A field once planted seldom needs planting again," she said. The rich round pumpkins would grow up among the corn and sell for about 75 cents a bushel. The various Indian tribes had been cultivating corn for centuries.

Wild honey was plentiful as was the beeswax which was sold in Mexico to make candles for the churches. And of course game was everywhere, deer, rabbit, squirrel, wild hogs, called "javelina," antelope, dove, quail, duck, bear and buffalo.

Food was definitely available for the taking. After that came the hard task of processing and cooking the bounty. That's where the women usually came in, although many women hunted as well. But as far as planting gardens in early Texas, that work fell to the women too. And like women the world over, they often added flowers.

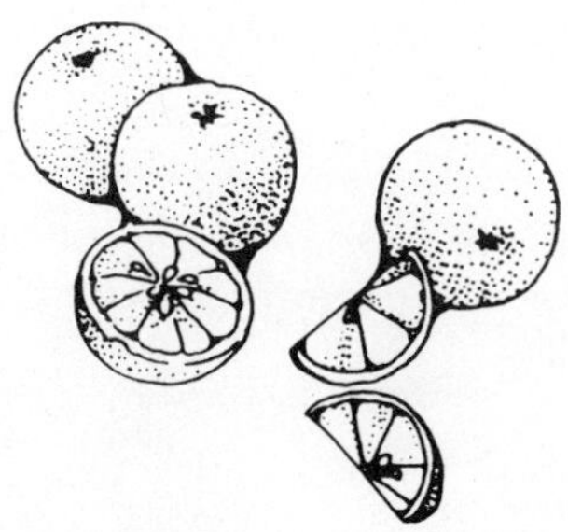

PREPARING GAME

Many of our receipts require fresh game. Preparing game varies some but the essentials are that you hang the animal head down, bleed it, skin the animal and remove the entrails as quickly as possible which is part of field dressing it. Usually a hunter will quarter a deer or bear as well, but this is more for ease of toting it out of the woods. There is not as much worry in cooler weather, but when it is hot, sometimes meat is put into a cool stream for a short time to help preserve it, though there is some argument about whether this is a good practice. To keep flies off the meat, the cook would wrap the fresh kill in clean muslin. Then she would put this into a straw-lined muslin flour sack and hang the sack in a cool dry place. When flies would light on the flower sack, the layer of straw kept them from reaching the meat. The sack could be used year after year if the cook washed it.

The main thing the cook does when the meat is brought to the kitchen is clean it in several waters until any blood, entrails or hair are all gone. Be sure the meat is not ruined. A favorite game in Texas was bear meat, particularly bear stew which needed to cook at least five hours or it would be too tough to eat. Of course, the women bought bear grease from the Indians and it was excellent to cook with, adding a rich flavor to steaks and fried potatoes. Bear grease was even used to oil guns.

BEAUTY TIPS FROM THE 1830s

Pioneer women worried about their appearance, but there were great difficulties carrying out personal toilettes, even for well-to-do women.

For women like Jane Long, there was precious little time for primping. Cooking was a full time job. Tending the house, taking care of children, boarders and livestock, kept women busy from dusk 'til dawn. Even so, each family made their own shampoo, toothpaste (toothpowder) and cosmetics.

Jane Long living in the West of the 1830's was a strikingly attractive woman. She was known for her beauty. Like many other women of her day, she might have used some of the following home-made beauty and health concoctions.

SHAMPOOS

#1 A compound for cleansing the hair is diluted ammonia water with 1 part of aqua ammonia to 10 parts of water. Rinse the hair and scalp with clear warm water after application.

#2 Pour 1 pint of boiling water on a handful of rosemary leaves, and add 1/2 tablespoonful of carbonate of ammonia. Cork tightly and let stand over night, shake well, and strain through a layer of heavy muslin. Preserve in a tightly stoppered bottle. Apply to wet hair. Rub into the scalp thoroughly and then rinse out with clear warm water.

#3 Possibly the best shampoo of all is made of the yolk of an egg beaten up with a pint of soft warm water. Apply at once, and rinse off with warm water and castile or other hard soap.

TOOTHPOWDERS

Chewing dry toast, crackers, hard bread and other coarse food aids in keeping the teeth in good condition. It is brushing that keeps teeth their healthiest. Toothpowders helped with cleaning, whitening and breath freshening. Toothpowders are varied, but have some common ingredients. Prepared chalk, bole (a clay-like substance found in the veins of various rocks), magnesia (as in milk of magnesia), and charcoal are just a few. Toothpowders were converted into pastes with the addition of a little clarified honey or almond cream.

Just moisten a toothbrush, dip in one of the powders and brush the teeth with an up and down motion. Rinse the mouth thoroughly with water when finished.

TO WASH THE FACE

When the face is red or dry from exposure to sun and air, or grimed with dirt or smoke it is adviseable to put on it a quantity of cold cream and rub thoroughly with a soft cloth. Fill a basin two-thirds full with fresh soft water. Dip the face in the water, and afterwards the hands. Soap the face well, and rub with a gentle motion over the face. Dip the face a second time, rinse thoroughly, and wipe with a clean soft, towel.

The effect of a clean face is altogether delightful. Such a bath tends to rest and refresh the bather and put her in a good temper.

SOAPS

Pure soaps do not irritate the skin. Soaps fall into two categories: those containing free alkali in the form of potash or soda lye, and the so-called neutral or fatty soaps. The former increase the swelling and softening of the horny parts of the skin. The latter are better adapted to persons of sensitive skin, although their detergent effects are not so marked. Some of the latter include castile, glycerin, curd soaps, and the like.

ROUGES AND FACE COSMETICS

Cold Creams

Cold cream is one of the most useful of preparations. Made from a variety of ingredients including white wax, almond oil, lard, suet, and distilled waters, essences or scented oils, it acts as a preventative and as a remedy for sunburn and reddening of the skin, chapped hands and lips, and frostbite (among other things).

To prepare cold cream melt 2 drams of white wax in a double boiler with 1 ounce of spermaceti, and 3 1/2 ounces of oil of sweet almonds. Remove from the fire and add in a continuous thin stream of 2 fluid ounces of rose water stirring constantly until cold.

Face Powders

For plain face powder without perfume, pure white cornstarch can hardly be improved upon.

For a scented powder mix together equal quantities of rice flour, fuller's earth, and cornstarch, and perfume with any essence or oil - rose, violet for example.

For a rose face powder mix 8 ounces of pulverized rose leaves with 4 ounces of pulverized sandalwood, and add 1 dram of the attar of roses.

Rouges

The base for rouge is usually French chalk, almond oil or animal fat colored with cochineal, carmine, vermilion or other red coloring matter. To Prepare Cochineal, take a small bit of cochineal (insect's shell). Lay it on a flat plate, bruise it with the blade of a knife. Put it into half a teacupful of spirits. Let it stand a quarter of an hour, and then filter it through fine muslin. Always ready for immediate use.

Mix 4 ounces of powdered French chalk with 2 drams of oil of almonds and 1 dram of powdered carmine.

Another rouge is made by taking a piece of unscented pomatum about the size of a pea, and placing on it a piece of carmine about the size of a pin head. Mix the two together and apply with a bit of cotton.

Rouge in liquid form is known as "bloom of youth," "bloom of roses," "almond bloom," etc. These preparations have distilled water or alcohol as a base. Color is added with Brazil wood, red sanders, cochineal and other red colorings.

Put in a glass fruit jar 4 ounces of finely powdered cochineal; add 4 ounces of water and the same amount of aqua ammonia; cover with a wet cloth and let simmer 3 or 4 hours in a double boiler. This preparation is ready for use as soon as it is cool.

REMEDIES FOR CHAPPED HANDS

These fall into two categories: solid unguents such as wax, lard, unsalted butter, mutton suet, bear grease, and the like; and liquid unguents such as glycerin, egg yolk, honey, almond oil, linseed oil and olive oil to name a few. These bases are improved with the addition of any of the following soothing elements: borax, bitter almonds, balsam of fir, camphor, sal soda, carbolic acid, quince seed, and oatmeal. Just add a little at a time to one of the unguents until you find the soothing concoction that works best on your hands.

*NOTE: Glycerin may be used pure or scented with any essential oil. Rub the hands at night with the same motion as when washing them. To soften and whiten the hands, use a mixture of two thirds glycerin and one third rose water.

MILK FOR THE SKIN

New milk, skimmed milk and buttermilk make useful and simple washes for the skin. When used daily they tend to make the skin soft, smooth, and white. Buttermilk is useful for freckles and acne, and relieves itching and local irritations of the skin. Pure, fresh cream is a simple and effective remedy for chapped hands and lips.

TO REMOVE FRECKLES

Acid preparations containing alum, lemon juice, horse-radish, buttermilk and the like, are effective in removing or lightening freckles. It must be said that these acidic preparations may be injurious to the skin if used frequently.

The best thing to do to freckles is no-thing.

HERBS FOR HOME REMEDIES

THE MEDICINE CLOSET

Even in the households of generally healthy families, a medicine closet should hold in reserve all sorts of simple medicines and emergency items. Keep the closet clean. Secure with a lock, keeping the key at the ready for emergencies. Divide the shelves into sections or compartments. Store everything that is poisonous in one section. In another section store gauze, cotton, linen, poultice bags, and so forth. Everyday remedies belong on a shelf of their own. These include camphor, calomel, castor oil, glycerin, Epsom salts as a cathartic, Jamaica ginger, sweet spirits of nitre, cascara sagrada, the bark of the cascara used as a laxative, and other roots and herbs believed to be helpful in the healing arts.

Keep antiseptics on another shelf. Also things for emergencies, such as alcohol, borax, charcoal, witch hazel, turpentine and peroxide.

Linen strips two to three inches wide should be kept on this shelf as well, after they are rolled up from end to end. Keep as many as will fit in a wide-mouthed fruit jar. Fill the top with absorbent cotton, set the jar upon a trivet in a kettle of cold water deep enough to have the water come nearly to the neck, and allow the water to come almost to the boiling point. The jar will need a weight laid across the top to hold it steady. Keep the water at about 180 degrees for three hours. Lift the jar off the kettle and let stand until the water becomes cold. Then take the jar out, screw the top on tightly and put away. The linen will then be so perfectly sterilized that in using it there will be no possible danger of infecting a fresh wound.

Also remember to keep small draughts of whiskey and brandy in the medicine closet for pain-relieving purposes.

HERBS GROWN IN TEXAS

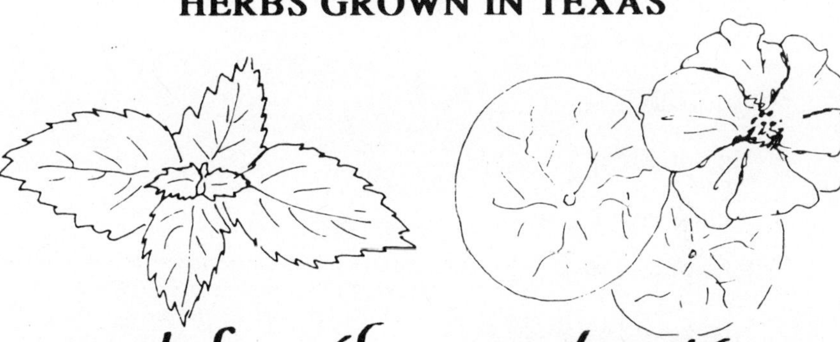

INDEX

A

B

BREADS

C

CAKES

CANDY

D

E

F

G

H

I

J

K

PIES

Q

R

S

T

V

W

NOTES:

JANE LONG'S
BRAZORIA INN

An Early Texas Cookbook

Our cookbook is available to Your organization at a special discount to use as a fundraiser.

For information, please call

Coldwater Press

Ph. 214.328.7612

Fax: 214.320.2480

email: JaneWLong@aol.com

Please send ______copies of Jane Long's Brazoria Inn

@ 9.95 each + 2.23 P&h + .82 TAX □ $12. TO:

Send to______________________________

(Address)____________________________

(City)________________State_____Zip________

Note: For more than 4 books, CWP will pay postage and handling.

Add only tax.

Checks to: Coldwater Productions, Inc.

9806 Coldwater Dallas, Tx 75228